SWEDISH GENIUS

© BOKFÖRLAGET MAX STRÖM 2003

© TEXT: PETTER KARLSSON AND JOHAN ERSÉUS

TRANSLATOR: KIM LOUGHRAN

GRAPHIC DESIGN: PATRIC LEO

LAYOUT: PETRA AHSTON INKAPÖÖL

EDITOR: CHARLOTTA BROADY

PICTURE EDITORS: SUSANNE REALI AND JAAK KRUUSMÄGI

FACT CHECKERS: SVANTE GUNNARSSON, URBAN KRONSTRÖM,

ERLAND SELLBERG AND KALLE WESTBERG

COLOUR SEPARATION, PRINTING AND BINDING: GRAPHICOM, ITALY 2003

ISBN 91-89204-36-0

SWEDISH GENIUS

TEXT PETTER KARLSSON. RESEARCH JOHAN ERSÉUS

CONTENTS

THE MEN WHO TRANSFORMED SWEDEN

The history of Swedish inventors is also the history of modern Sweden. Inventors played a decisive role in the progress of industrialism in Sweden and their inventions lynchpinned a number of successful companies. Further, their work was preparation for a lengthy global success ride for Swedish quality.

Looking at history through the prism of dates, you might conclude that Sweden became a modern nation in 1809. That is also when Sweden got its first, formal constitutional laws, including a new structure for government.

The war with Russia (1808–09) was rife with dramatic incidents, including the loss of Finland to Russia, and there was drama in the subsequent dethronement of King Gustav IV Adolf and the import of a French marshal as replacement king. But history's real shifts are seldom dramatic; Sweden remained itself and a new war replaced the loss of Finland with Norway, in a union widely unappreciated in that latter country, which led to the dissolution of the union in 1905. This happened without armed hostilities and Sweden has thus enjoyed unbroken peace for two centuries.

In the early years of the 19th century, Bishop Esaias Tegnér noted that the nation flourished thanks to peace, potatoes and vaccine, and that the population was growing – almost doubling in his lifetime to 3.5 million at his death in 1846. A century later, the figure was seven million.

The vaccine Tegnér praised was against smallpox. By the end of the 19th century, enough had been learned about hygiene and the spread of disease that the risk for cholera epidemics was over, although at the beginning of the century, cities were still periodically ravaged.

For some time into the 20th century, there were still occasional famines in parts of the country but they quickly became rare. The spread of hospitals and improved hygiene, health care and diet all contributed to the huge rise in population.

The great period for industrialisation was in the decades around the turn of the 20th century and up until the First World War. In a period of 25 years, the contribution of industry to the Gross National Product doubled, surpassing that of agriculture. But from another perspective, Sweden would long remain an agrarian society. The cities were small. In 1820, Stockholm had a population of only 75,000. By 1900, it had grown to 300,000 and by mid-century, to 735,000. So industrialisation began late in Sweden and most Swedes still lived and worked in the country. Even at the time of the First World War, half of the population was involved in agriculture; not until the Second World War would more Swedes make a living from industry than farming.

Even in politics, Sweden was long managed by farmers and with the interests of agriculture chiefly in mind. In 1866, a representation reform gave Sweden a dual-chamber parliament, dominated by farmers and forestry owners.

Yet it was in these very years, from the mid-19th century and 100 years on, that numerous Swedes won international acclaim for significant inventions, which led in turn to the foundation of large and profitable companies such as ASEA, Volvo, SKF, Ericsson and many others. Without these enterprises, the welfare model that took shape between the wars and became Sweden's hallmark would not have been possible. There is a strong argument that the modern history of this country belongs to its inventors.

This book is about Swedish inventors. They cannot be portrayed as clichéd heroes or pioneers. At times, their success was due more to chance than to superiority over their fellows. But their ideas were converted to finished products and in many cases they contributed to the creation of successful companies.

This was a period of Swedish history when engineers took centre stage. Up until the end of the 19th century, industrial production was simply large-scale artisanship. Products were developed through trial and error: one solution after the other was tried out until after years of such testing an optimal solution was found. Products and machines were developed not on the drawing board but through practical testing. Before Nobel had produced a form of dynamite that was safe to use, there had been several accidents and victims. The same held true for Gustaf Dalén, who tested his inventions himself. L.M. Ericsson bothered little with theory and academic degrees, choosing to try things out instead, just as Janne Lundström had done earlier, in his quest for a safer match.

The connection to artisanship is also apparent in that most of these inventions were born from a need to solve a practical problem. When Sven Wingquist fashioned his ball-bearings it was through irritation with machines with single-row bearings that performed poorly and often broke down. Production time could be won if he could find a solution. And find it he did, which led in turn to the creation of a large industrial company.

Thomas Edison described the process of invention as 'Genius is one percent inspiration and 99 percent perspiration'. In other words: a rigorous, practical job. Inventors dedicated more sweat to their work than thought and analysis. They learned to systematise their testing, painstakingly working through variables to see what needed to be changed and what could be retained – a practice known to researchers as systematic parametric variation.

On the other hand, inventors are seldom visionaries, nor are they researchers testing laws of nature. When they do seek, the results can be absurd. Baltzar von Platen is thus the odd man out, fitting only partly the normal inventor profile. His development of the refrigerator followed the inventor's standard path from tangible, practical problem through ideas and tests to solution. But when, in the oil crisis of the 1970s, he proclaimed that the development of a perpetual motion machine was feasible, he contradicted the laws of nature and was dismissed as a loony by the scientific establishment. Had he been able to produce his perpetual motion machine, needing no energy input, his triumph would have been immense, but he had no more luck than the alchemists of a previous age who failed at changing metal to gold. Von Platen's energy machine was a total flop.

His example shows the need to separate natural and technical science from invention. Links do exist, but inventors are not researchers out to understand Nature; they are out to solve practical problems and use knowledge as a means to achieve their goals.

The word 'inventor' comes from Latin's 'invenire', meaning to 'come into'. This contains the element of surprise, of stumbling into something. There is a difference between inventing and discovering; in the latter, there is something waiting to be found, whereas what an inventor must find is far more hidden from our eyes.

What then is specific for an inventor? We have already established that his departure point is a practical problem. In modern economic terms, inventors are market-driven. Leonardo da Vinci is sometimes described as a visionary inventor who developed the principles of the flying machine and the parachute long before others. But had he not also been a brilliant artist, both he and his technical ideas would surely have been forgotten. There was neither the demand for his inventions nor the possibility of putting them to use.

An excellent example of this mechanism is the invention of the safety match. The ability to make fire and use it has been an integral part of civilisation since before antiquity. But it was not before the growth of industrialism with large cities and a new mode of living that the earlier, more complicated and dangerous production of fire seemed impractical and bothersome. Within a few decades, the problem was solved.

It took some time to abandon the principle of artisanship in invention. But incontestably, the organised technical education of engineers and increased specialisation made inventors more sector-focused and thrust them into closer contact with technical research. Gustaf de Laval was before his time in creating a kind of laboratory for experiments. He was himself an educated man with a PhD from 1872.

One might wonder whether inventors are driven by something inaccessible to others. What is it that makes a person – seemingly at any price and sometimes at any cost in money or energy – seek to solve problems? Certainly, many inventors have dreamt of a good monetary reward for their efforts but many appear to have largely the same intellectual motivation as theoretical researchers. It was scarcely a desire for riches or worldly fame that made Gustaf Dalén put his own life and that of others at risk. With many inventors, there is an inkling of a strong, idealistic dream of helping their fellow man.

Among the inventors in the book, some did become wealthy through their work. Both L.M. Ericsson and Sven Wingquist founded industrial empires that still exist. Others lost interest in the work once it became successful. Gustaf de Laval, for example, was hardly a financial genius and seemed to be driven more by conviction and purpose than by interest in income.

Since inventions are so closely connected to practical problems, it is not surprising that there have been frequent discussions over their authorship. Practically every inventor's products have been challenged.

This is, however, in the nature of things, since the problems inventors tackle are of interest to many and some of the possible solutions are also common knowledge. On the other hand, an inventor can be a lone wolf, and also be happy to be seen as a loner.

Inventors are heroes who are not only stubborn, systematic and perhaps brilliant; they also need luck. Nonetheless, it is the result that counts, not the brainwave.

An inventor named Gustaf Erik Pasch was in fact first to patent a safety match, but at the time, 1844, it was not possible to manufacture matches on a profitable scale. Justifiably, Janne Lundström is known as the real inventor of the safety match. He invented a marketable, usable match. And justifiably, his brother Carl deserves notice. For as we have established, invention is more than the theoretical solution to a current practical problem but also to make it actually work — the integral, entrepreneurial side of invention.

This is substantially different from scientific research where the idea is all that matters. Invention cannot be separated from execution: the result. It was not before dynamite was of practical use and therefore saleable that it became a real industrial invention; the same held true for the AGA lighthouse. And a zipper is fairly uninteresting as a concept; only when it proved its worth in trousers and skirts did it achieve a value.

Thus, the never-ending discussions over authorship are often fuelled by the bitter recriminations of those who feel cheated. One Hjalmar Ellström, for example, grieved on his deathbed over the accomplishments of his partner, C.E. Johansson. Even if Ellström really did originate the idea of gauge blocks — and even went further, as many have claimed — Johansson's energy and purpose were needed to fine-tune and market the invention.

And if Wingquist had not been lucky enough to be confronted with a stubbornly malfunctioning machine, he might never have invented the double-wheeled ball-bearing. Presumably, someone else would have done — a German or a Frenchman perhaps. But the Swede was first and thereby a large ball-bearing factory came to be built in Gothenburg. Which provided the pre-conditions for the Volvo car factory in the same city. Wingquist was a board member of the Volvo company from its inception. It would be difficult to visualise Sweden's 20th-century industrial history without those two factories.

In this light, it is important to recognise the significance of patents. Without them, inventors cannot be compensated for their work. The system of patenting was first developed in England. Until long into the 19th century, Sweden had a faulty system that, for example, prevented foreigners from owning patents for Sweden. Towards the end of that century, a new system was legislated for and, largely intact, still exists. It even covers other countries, although patents must still formally be applied for in each country. Only after patent approval does the inventor own his invention and the assurance of possible profit.

The safety match was invented by a poetry-writing humanist and the telephone was developed by an autodidact farmer's son in the old artisan way. But by the turn of the 20th century, inventing had become more the province of engineers. Apace with specialisation in industry, where engineers had made inroads in the preceding decades, problems too become specialised. It was no longer simple for an uneducated person to solve problems by pure ingenuity.

It is striking how great a role the United States has played in the education and even in the background of Swedish inventors. Most of them spent time, lengthy or otherwise, on the American continent, even if their studies took them to other countries as well. As communications improved, these journeys became even easier.

John Ericsson meant a great deal to other Swedish inventors. He was responsible for many inventions of his own, but he was primarily a role model. Certainly, he contributed to Swedish inventors' interest in the American market. Another factor was the contact that Swedish inventors had with each other.

Most Swedish inventors came from humble environments, their youth marked by sacrifice and hard work. With success, they continued to honour their puritan values. There are exceptions to the rule, but it is interesting to note that few of them remained industrialists for life. Many surrendered responsibility for their inventions and their companies; it seems almost that most Swedish inventors were never at home with the duties of running a company.

Although the greatest entrepreneur among them, Carl Lundström, was just that, but even he, along with L.M. Ericsson of telephone fame, had become a farmer by the end of the 19th century. For us, this might appear to be a retreat from industrialised society to agrarian values. But Lundström had, for a short while, been a member of parliament and had seen better than most the status and power of the farmers. Becoming the owner of a large property was thus a career move. Industrialisation was still at the stage where prominent industrialists could leave their companies to become farmers.

The history of Swedish inventors can be seen in the light of international developments in a period when industrialisation was formative for nations. It became a national obligation to support new inventions, which were seen as primarily contributions to the progress of Swedish industry. The safety match was promoted as a Swedish invention that would profile the nation at the great Paris World Fair of 1867. Such exhibitions were opportunities for inventors and industrialists to network but were also a prompt for governments to encourage innovations.

Thus, the hundred years from the mid-19th century forward are the story of national industrialisation in an international context. But also the story of a time when a lone inventor, with little access to laboratories and materials, was still able to conquer markets with only the result of his own creative efforts. In both respects, our world has changed.

Erland Sellberg,
Associate Professor in the History of Ideas, Stockholm University.

SPREADER OF LIGHT

Gustaf Dalén 1869–1937

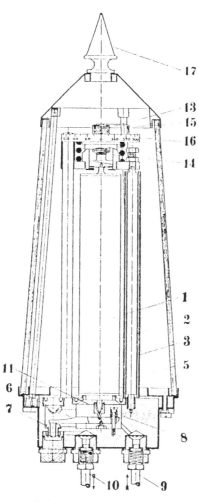

Solventil i genomskärning.

'Let him have one of my eyes!' the man cried.

'I'm serious! Give the boss one of my eyes, so he can see again.'

It was an incredible gesture. Gustaf Dalén lay in a hospital bed with a mangled body and ruined eyesight and outside stood one of his employees, cap in hand, begging the doctor to transplant his own eye.

For obvious ethical and medical reasons, it was impossible. And perhaps the words were not exactly those quoted above; the origin of the story is obscure and has presumably been recast and embroidered. The interesting part is what the anecdote reveals of the sudden emotional tumult that resulted when the inventor of the AGA lighthouse, Managing Director Gustaf Dalén, on 27 September 1912 became the victim of his own dreams of light and was banished to the darkness he had always battled.

This is the crux of the story: light and darkness. Shining steel and blackened rods. Mysterious flashes from a blacked-out apartment on Kungstensgatan street in Stockholm and a redemptive chain of lighthouses along the world's darkest, most feared seafaring channels.

The accident: a terrible explosion in a quarry site, when a broken pressure gauge fooled one of the country's sharpest minds into approaching a gas cylinder that had been heated red-hot over a log fire.

All Dalén's biographers, however, agree that the compassionate worker actually existed. The eye specialist at the Serafimer General Hospital in Stockholm where Dalén was taken was, by amazing coincidence, Dalén's own brother, Albin, who was apparently contacted by a grey-faced and teary-eyed AGA employee, begging the doctor to do everything in his power to help 'poor boss'.

There was a factory-floor rumour that one of Dalén's eyes could be saved by a new American operating method. A healthy cornea could be used to replace the one shattered by the blast. But a martyr would be needed, an almost inhuman sacrifice. It is not inconceivable that a sensitive person could get carried away by the emotional turmoil.

It was quickly established that the other eye could not be saved.

An exploding acetylene cylinder is a scatter bomb of fire and iron. When the accident occurred, Dalén was standing within half a metre. He did not have a chance. When smoke settled in the quarry, most of his co-workers believed they were looking at the body of a dead man. But when they bent down to the bloodied face, someone noticed he

The man who conquered darkness. Gustaf Dalén (1869–1937) was blinded in an explosion trial gone wrong. This picture was taken for an informal, at-home interview in his white stone residence on suburban Stockholm's genteel Lidingö Island. He had been sightless for more than 16 years. The journalist's report breathlessly described the famous inventor's skilful guided tour through a house had had never seen completed.

Previous page: Gustaf Dalén's revolutionary sun valve, in use from 1907.

17

was still breathing. Before the ambulance arrived, Dalén had said farewell to his colleagues and asked Dr Nyström: 'With whom have I the honour of speaking?' Offered morphine, Dalén declined, saying he wanted his head to be clear 'when I say goodbye to my wife'.

He was almost frighteningly calm, witnesses said.

It may have been the effect of the shock. But Gustaf Dalén also seemed to be a man who possessed singular spiritual strength that would guide him around reefs and rocks throughout his life.

Farmer Dalén's boy, from Stenstorp in the southern province of Västergötland, was a problem-solver. He thrived on tackling predicaments. As an inventor, he was an almost Jungian archetype, a relic from the teachings of Plato, imaginative and pragmatic at the same time. He had sweeping vision but his solutions were so simple that it was astonishing no one had discovered them before. He made courageous leaps in reasoning, but took pains to show patience, to make measured progress, to apply for patents only after his inventions had been tested at almost ridiculous length.

The blinking light at 52, Kungstensgatan street was an example.

Gustaf Dalén's first 'flashing apparatus' – an ingenious idea involving a pulsating membrane that released small bubbles of gas to a pilot flame, igniting them – was left to blink away for months in the Dalén family apartment before it was deemed ready for release to the world.

A gas-fired lighthouse had long been every seaman's dream, since its beam was considerably more clear than that produced by kerosene. The problem was the blinking. The heat produced was insufficient to power the shield that interrupted the light. Gustaf Dalén realised he was sitting on a fortune. When the police pounded on his door one night, Dalén feared that something had happened to his parents at their country home. Later, after the constable and the curious crowd on the street had been mollified to hear that the suspected blaze was in fact a new invention, Dalén began to worry that someone might have seen too much. He had become accustomed to drawing the blinds but had forgotten on this occasion, and a few inebriated strollers had apparently been drawn, moth-like, to the flare.

Gustaf Dalén was used to attracting attention.

Years after his death, at the September 1954 première of the film 'Victory in the Dark' in Dalén's home town of Stenstorp, older villagers emerged from the cinema darkness with anecdotes that the film

Let there be light! Axel Nordvall, one of Gustaf Dalén's closest colleagues at the AGA company, balances proudly on one of the light buoys made to guide seamen over inky seas.

had missed. A television reporter interviewing the aged Charlotta Larsson was told how she 'fainted right off' when the 15-year-old Gustaf suddenly appeared astride a home-made velocipede with iron wheels.

More famous is the story of his first invention, an alarm clock that ingeniously lit a kerosene lamp and heated a coffee pot before waking its owner. Gustaf's father, Anders, had bought the clock at an auction and Gustaf put it in working order. He then equipped the clock with a sandpaper-clad pulley that started to rotate at a certain hour. A phosphorous match on a moveable arm was positioned against the pulley. When the match was lit, the arm would turn and light the wick of an oil lamp. Over this was a pot of coffee, prepared the previous evening. A quarter of an hour later, the alarm would ring to wake the sleeper.

Reminiscing in his later years about the alarm clock, Dalén said the idea sprang from his three greatest needs: 'I was very interested in mechanics, very slow in the mornings, and very fond of coffee.'

Asked by his father to shell some peas, Gustaf simply attached a belt to a threshing machine and sat back, twiddling his thumbs, while the shelled peas tumbled into a bucket. Reminiscing in his later years about the alarm clock, Dalén said the idea sprang from his three greatest needs: 'I was very interested in mechanics, very slow in the mornings, and very fond of coffee.'

Throughout his life, he would be dependent on at least ten hours of sleep a night. He even had plans for an inspired system of ropes and pulleys that would jerk away two supports under a bed, throwing a late-sleeper to the floor. His brother Hjalmar vehemently vetoed the idea. (Hjalmar was to become a lawyer, and already had a potent way with words.)

The Dalén family's beautiful homestead, Skräddargården, is still standing, close by the railway line. Young Gustaf used to hide letters under the carriages to communicate with his brothers down the line in Skara, thereby saving on stamps. To the right of the homestead's veranda is an ash that is leafier than any other tree near the house.

'It was where Gustaf and the other men used to relieve themselves. The tree apparently almost died in the beginning, but revived and is now the only surviving ash on the property.'

This is according to the current owner, Britt Högrell, whose

As a fifteen-year-old, Dalén frightened the daylights out of the local biddies with a velocipede on rattling, beaten-iron wheels. A few years later, Gustaf Dalén courted his wife-to-be, Elma, on another home-made vehicle, equipped with his unique brake system.

grandfather Julius moved into the homestead's northern wing in 1889. The Dahlén family (the ever-rational Gustaf later dispensed with the 'h') had already lived there for 20 years. Gustaf was born in the kitchen in 1869, the year the main building was completed.

His old room, 15 steps up, is unchanged, with a view over the lush garden, where Gustaf planted bushes in oval configurations, put down currants and laid circular paths, all in the English style. Two boys' beds are still positioned with their foot-ends closest to the white tile oven. The famous alarm clock is by the window.

'Gustaf Dalén visited occasionally when he was old. I remember him walking into this room; it must have been in the mid-1920s. Suddenly, a dark figure was standing there in the doorway – he was dressed in black and wore dark glasses – and said, "How small the room is! And to think we used to call it the big room." How could he judge the size of the room, since he was blind? He must have been able to sense the air pressure, or maybe he went by the echo.'

Gustaf Dalén's favourite flower appears to have been the sunflower. When his mother, Lovisa, was on her deathbed in 1890 at the Serafimer General Hospital, she stroked his cheek and whispered, 'Be the sun's friend.' She could hardly know how perspicacious she was.

But for the young Gustaf, the flourishing vegetation and the billowing fields were mainly a source of torment. His four siblings had already left home to pursue studies. Gottfrid was to become a church dean, Albin a professor of ophthalmology, Hildur a teacher and Hjalmar a lawyer. Their father's plan was for the tyke to take over the farm. And hadn't Bergqvist the village teacher said, 'Gustaf won't amount to anything'?

The 'good-for-nothing' opened a seed shop and a dairy to augment his income. And at the age of 21, Gustaf Dalén was to see his first mechanical workshop, and the sight of it would forever be in his dreams. It annoyed him that a farmer was paid as much for thin milk as for rich, so he built a butterfat-content meter of his own design in a shed. Trusting to the gods and with a proper lunchbox, Dalén journeyed to Stockholm and asked for an audience with the renowned Gustaf de Laval, industrialist and inventor of the centrifugal separator. De Laval muttered, 'Extraordinary, very extraordinary,' and rummaged in a cupboard to find the blueprints and patent for his own, newly invented butterfat-content meter, called the butyrometer.

He was meant to be a farmer like his father. But Gustaf Dalén never got used to dung heaps and the like, and would frequently disappear into a shed to build inventions: the alarm clock that also prepared his morning coffee, a thresher for peas and a device for measuring butterfat content.

Gustaf Dalén's childhood home, where his mother gave birth to Gustaf on a kitchen bench. In season, the garden would be full of his favourite sunflowers. To the right of the veranda is the ash that almost died from popularity – it was the favourite spot for Gustaf and the other males on the farm to relieve themselves.

Gustaf Dalén went back home to his 50 acres with mixed feelings. Gustaf de Laval's butterfat meter was obviously first, but it was a more complicated machine. On top of that, the Great Man had terminated the interview by scribbling a few hieroglyphics on a business card and bidding Dalén to come back when he was properly educated. 'Since without education, one's growth is stunted. But when you return, I will have forgotten what I said; my head is filled with so much else. Take this card and present it to me when you come back, so that my memory will be refreshed.'

His irascible father had, however, no money to lend Gustaf, who was forced to turn to his father-in-law-to-be, farmer Persson of Munkabo. When Gustaf finally started his studies at the Chalmers Institute of Technology in Göteborg, he was all of 27 years old. He grumbled about being 'an old fogey' who couldn't learn things and wasn't good at foreign languages.

But Gustaf started to learn.

In fact, he learned so much that, in 1896, he was awarded a Chalmers scholarship and went on to the Polytechnikum in Zurich and shortly afterwards found himself once more in the Swedish capital, as an employee working on de Laval's turbine experiments. He was already running an after-hours engineering company together with a fellow student, Henrik von Celsing, an eccentric youth once seen leading a tame moose through central Stockholm.

Dalén and Celsing worked with the currently fashionable acetylene gas. Whoever could find out how to avert explosions could expect to make a fortune. The kitchen in Dalén's apartment was swiftly converted into a laboratory. The ceiling was soon blackened with soot and had to be repainted. Dalén did the rounds of country towns, trying to convince city fathers to light their streets and heat their buildings with the gas, since 'acetylene provides an attractive light, not unlike the sun's'.

In 1904, a limited company, Aktiebolaget Gasaccumulator or AGA, was started, and immediately began to expand, thanks to Dalén's brainwaves.

Since 1901, Gustaf had been settled down with Elma, the sister of a pal from military service days, Pers Persson. Fourteen previously, he had fallen off a bicycle and into her arms on a country road in Västergötland province. She was blunt with her demands: 'I'm not

He fell off his bike right into her arms. Gustaf Dalén was 32 when he married farm girl Elma Persson. Their marriage was extraordinarily successful in many ways. Elma's father even lent Gustaf money for university studies when Gustaf's own father refused.

Dalén's first partner, Henrik von Celsing was an eccentric who delighted in walking his tame elk Lotta through the Stockholm streets. One winter, a race was arranged, pitting Lotta against a trotting horse and a car on the ice close to the city centre. But when the starting gun was fired, Lotta simply sat down. "Smart animal!" commented von Celsing.

marrying a bumpkin farmer!' 'What about an engineer?' he pleaded. 'All right. That's different!'

It was a happy marriage, with an issue of four well-behaved children. In a magazine interview many years later, Gustaf was to say, 'Marriage is a lottery and I've won first prize,' with Elma adding: 'There's no one else like Gustaf, not as a person, a husband or a father.'

The story goes that Elma's job as a maid for a wealthy family led Gustaf straight to chief engineer John Höyer.

'So, you work with gas?' said Höyer. 'Then it's odd that none of you has been able to invent an acetylene-lit lighthouse, with the fine flame acetylene gives.'

'How frequent does the flashing have to be?' Dalén asked. 'Can it be really fast?'

'The faster the better, to make it more visible.'

Exit promising young inventor; enter, later, celebrated inventor with a world-beating invention. All one summer, a strange lighthouse prototype could be seen flashing from Skeppsholmen islet in central Stockholm. When the Daléns, now with their own home help, took a walk down to the water, Gustaf would point and say: 'Elma, that thing is going to make us money!'

Between 1905 and 1908, Gustaf Dalén came up with the four mainstays of AGA's world renown:

1. the flashing apparatus, the ingenious device with the pulsating membrane and gas bubbles, installed in 5,000 buoys and lighthouses between 1906 and 1918
2. AGA mass, similar to Alfred Nobel's dynamite cartridges, a sparkling silica mass that absorbed acetylene, making accumulators impact-resistant and reducing the risk of explosion
3. the sun valve, a black metal rod that expanded two thousandths of a millimetre in daylight, thereby blocking a gas valve
4. the Dalén Mixer, which mixed gas and air to the right proportions, thus increasing the brightness of a beacon

Perhaps the sun valve was the most astonishing, in all its genial simplicity. Hearing of it, the great Edison fulminated: 'It won't work!' When told it was already in operation, he interrupted his informant, repeating: 'It will not function!'

The German patent office said the same, dismissing the blueprints

The flashing apparatus or cut-off valve, to the left, worked through the regular release of gas bubbles through a membrane, creating a blinking beam when ignited. When Gustaf Dalén tested it at home in his apartment, worried neighbours called the police.

The sun valve, to the right, was based on the simple phenomenon of a metal rod warming in daylight and expanding by two thousandths of a millimetre – enough to close another valve and thereby save the considerable volume of gas unneeded in daytime.

For almost a century, AGA's beacons have spread light across the globe – as here, on a reef at Habushiva, Japan in the early 1920s.

Next page: illuminated minds at the AGA design office in Stockholm in about 1910. Gustaf Dalén was a demanding but popular boss, with an ability to spot talent among aspiring young engineers.

as 'ausgeschlossen!' Out of the question! Upon hearing this, Dalén hastened south by train, strode into the patent office, assembled his apparatus on a table and asked the gentlemen present to please draw the curtains. When light flooded in, the valve closed. When the curtains were again closed, the valve reopened within seconds.

'How much gas does it save?' someone asked.

'Ninety-four per cent,' answered Dalén.

'But that is …' (pause) '… very good!'

In 1912, the lighthouse at the seaward tip of Stockholm's large park island, Djurgården, became the first in the world to use a sun valve. (When the lighthouse was electrified 68 years later, it was noted that the valve had never needed repair.) But the real leap was of course in 1912 when orders worth millions started pouring in for the newly dug Panama Canal. With every passing day, a new gas flame was lit somewhere along the world's shipping lanes. Every new day, massive new orders arrived at the AGA factory.

And Gustaf Dalén was rapidly inventing ingenious improvements: lead balls that melted to stop an explosion in a pipe impacting a gas mixer; an automatic incandescent mantle changer that allowed a beacon to service itself for a year at a time.

He was prospering, this landlubber now making the seas navigable. The family's new house was being built on the exclusive island-suburb of Lidingö. It was a palace in white stone, but in which 'no room is to be too fancy for a pillow fight'.

At the nearby factory, the workers seemed to stand to attention in his presence. Dalén was said to be a good, albeit demanding, boss. While the company thrived, he had roomy barracks built for his workers on lush slopes; he set up pension funds and communal dining facilities; he reserved space for the employees' vegetable allotments; he purchased suckling pigs at a discount; he opened the Red Owl Cinema and he successfully lobbied the authorities to extend tram and steamboat routes.

He involved himself in a number of issues, among them the abandoning of the gold standard.

'It's madness to risk people's lives down in the gold mines,' he growled, adding with a grin:

'But gold is a fine material – resilient and almost imperishable. Undeniably useful for roofing.'

An advertisement from 1911. AGA was once again a prospering enterprise, after nearly going bankrupt in connection with a general strike two years earlier.

Money poured in when the company won a huge order from the newly built Panama Canal in the 1910s.

The 'sorcerers' workshop' in 1906. Gustaf Dalén's colleagues are experimenting with the revolutionary AGA Mass – a method of binding gas into more manageable silica, thereby reducing the risk of explosions.

Next page: An age of enlightenment. AGA's new factory on Lidingö island was an ultra modern facility in several ways. Gustaf Dalén started an employee-welfare programme, helping staff with housing and retirement funds. He even bought piglets for the factory and opened a cinema for employees.

Glänsande och synnerligen löftesrik uppfinnarbana stäckad af den svåra explosionsolyckan vid Alby

En kort resumé af direktör Daléns uppfinningar, hvilka förskaffat honom ett berömdt namn öfver hela världen.

En lysboj och fyrskeppet Svinbådan, båda med Aga-klippljus.

Den svåra explosionsolyckan vid Alby, för hvilkens förlopp å annat ställe i dagens tidning närmare redogöres, har spridt sorg och förstämning i vida kretsar, ty den har hårdast

Politically, he was to drift to the right, noticeably after 1909, when AGA barely survived a general strike and he was talked into becoming a managing director at a handsome salary. Up until then, he had been merely a well-paid star engineer. But now, the consortium of businessmen from Västergötland province that came to AGA's rescue made it conditional that their provincial compatriot Dalén be at the helm.

'I'm no businessman,' protested Dalén modestly, but let slip that he had made his first money selling lead pencils in the school playground, after first cycling from the farm to Skara to buy them in bulk.

And, fortuitously, the economy began to recover. In 1910, AGA again picked up speed, now with a new master. Gas welding, which Dalén was the first Swede to test, at Finnboda shipyards in 1902, was a new winner. The farmer's son from Stenstorp was enjoying life.

'I smoke like a chimney, but never touch alcohol,' he observed with satisfaction, as the number of cigars smoked increased.

Then came the fateful day, 27 September 1912 – a bright, clear day.

On a property near Stockholm belonging to his friend and fellow-inventor, Lars Magnus Ericsson, in a quarry planned to house a laundry, the fifth gas cylinder was still intact, hissing, after the others had exploded over the fire.

The experiment was partly a consequence of the Panama contract: How would gas cylinders react in a hot climate? Would they explode? Dalén needed to know. When cylinder number five refused to explode, he and chemist Arvid Gyllsdorff inched slowly forward. Gyllsdorff had a mineral water bottle in one hand, to collect leaking gas for analysis. Dalén was right beside him.

'Be careful sir,' someone called.

'It's all right. We're just going to collect some gas.'

Gyllsdorff reaches forward with the bottle …

These days, Swedish fire prevention rules impose a 300-metre safety zone around an AGA gas cylinder in a fire situation. Gustaf Dalén was standing right next to an explosion that made the night heave and the sound be heard for tens of kilometres. He was thrown to the ground, his clothes ablaze from the burning gas. His face was bloody, his hands roasted. There was a hole where one of his eyes used to be.

'I feel it's the end,' whispered Dalén. 'Tell my family goodbye.'

And when told that the others had survived unscathed: 'That makes me happy.'

This scene is the last Gustaf Dalén would ever see. Dalén, in the bowler hat and closest to the camera, is testing gas tubes at the Ericsson telephone company's own quarry on 27 September 1912. Barely a minute after the picture was snapped, one of the tubes would explode in his face and rip through his eyes. The tragic accident generated metres of newsprint in the following day's papers.

To read newspaper accounts from the following days, when Dalén was in critical condition, is like following the script of an American soap opera:

- assistant, clothes ablaze, succeeds in stifling the flames with his own hands
- doctor struggling to save his brother's life goes grey in two weeks
- despairing wife hears her husband say: 'Elma, our journey is at an end. I so wanted to see our children grow up.'
- will dictated at hospital bedside
- AGA shares plunge
- And, of course, the worker who offered to sacrifice one of his own eyes for his boss and who instantly became a hero of mythological proportions.

The story of Dalén's journey into darkness had all the ingredients: hope, despair, courage, tragedy and – like a well-rehearsed finale – his Nobel Prize, the news coming at half past nine in the evening of 12 November, with the great man sightless and ravaged in the infirmary.

Not that he was unqualified. Undeniably, his inventions were brilliant and had 'conferred … benefit on mankind'. But was it just an incredible coincidence that he was given the prize only a month after the accident that almost took his life?

We will probably never know. The most relevant document is perhaps a letter sent to the wounded Dalén by Science Academician Sven Hedin, in which he enthusiastically described the euphoria that followed another academician's mention of Dalén's name. 'With your light of genius, you have illuminated the shipping channels of our entire globe,' wrote Hedin. 'You are saving innumerable lives now and for the future.'

At the Dalén Museum in Stenstorp, the district's favourite son had virtually been sainted. 'When does he stand up?' asked children when shown the wax dummy, sitting with its dark glasses amidst wondrous objects. In the entry hall were scrawled children's drawings of lighthouses and blind men. Display cabinets were crowded with flashing apparatuses, airport beacons and traffic lights. The local cinema showed 'Victory in Darkness'. ('The students from Chalmers come here to sob.') The box office had for sale gold 'optimist badges' –

A gas-powered semaphore and an early traffic light on Stockholm's central Kungsgatan street. Dalén thought his inventions could be of use even on dry land.

copies of the ones Dalén had ordered engraved following the crash of the Kreuger match empire; he had a bunch of them stuck behind his lapel, handy for dispensing to moaners.

Gustaf Dalén's story is, most of all, about one man's astounding inner strength.

To never give up. To defy the dark and, instead, bring light. To rise up from a sickbed, two months after personal tragedy, and fling oneself again at the unsolved mysteries of existence.

'You hardly think about his blindness when you see him at work,' wrote J.H. Nauckhoff, a fellow engineer, in a graceful monograph on Dalén published in 1927. 'He moves easily and insouciantly, and takes the arm of his guide apparently more as in confidence than in need. He manages his office's three telephones with no trouble at all, sometimes conversing on two of them at once.'

'I shall still have my thoughts, come what may, and if I cannot myself see, I can always find someone intelligent to draw the plans, as long as my ideas are clear.'

This was Gustaf Dalén, speaking to an interviewer in his unmistakably Västergötland-accented Swedish, and declaring that the blind are more able to concentrate as 'many extraneous irritants disappear.

'Besides, it could have been worse. I could have lost my hearing and not been able to hear my wife's voice or the singing of birds.'

Despite his blindness, Dalén continued to throw parties and masquerades in the villa he never saw completed. His four children took turns in helping Dad around the house. On the veranda, Elma read to him from the newspapers and from 'Wonderful Swedish Lives' magazine. Down at the jetty, he found out where the water is deepest and then dived in, head first.

'With time, we learned to be very neat. We never left doors ajar and never left toys on the floor. Upstairs, there was a motorised treadway. He and Mother used to take a walk on it every evening, and then go to bed after the ten o'clock news,' said his young daughter, Inga-Lisa, not long ago. She remembered, too, how she and her father would skate on the harbour ice.

'Actually, dad preferred travelling to hot places, like Egypt or the Canaries. He came to visit me after I had moved to Cape Town. He really appreciated travel, even though he couldn't see. We never gave his blindness much thought. Dad was Dad. A wonderful father.'

Out walking with wife Elma outside their Lidingö Island home in 1937. Throughout life, Dalén showed unusual strength of character. Despite his handicap, he continued to run his company, ice-skate, throw parties and dive headfirst into the sea from his jetty.

After match king Ivar Kreuger's sensational bankruptcy early in the Depression, Swedes slumped into gloom – everyone except Gustaf Dalén, who made up Optimist pins that he handed out to everyone. His own was prominently displayed on his lapel.

Gustaf Dalén consented to several 'at-home' interviews. One reporter wrote that he had been piloted 'up a broad staircase, past heavy furniture in large rooms, without [Dalén] ever once groping for a footing. He took me out onto a sun-drenched terrace overlooking the glittering waters of the harbour, threw out his arms and said, "Isn't the view grand!"'

In February 1913, he expressed his gratitude to his employees by giving them an extra weekly wage. On the occasion, he said in an interview, 'I am totally recovered. Well, of course, one eye is missing and I'm still as blind as a bat in the other. Darkness does bring difficulties, but not so great that one can't master them and work almost as well as before.'

Even little Stenstorp was remembered. Dalén sent cash grants to industrious students, and, 'He lavished touching interest especially on the old and needy in his home town; his annual visits were the highlight of their lives,' wrote the reverential Nauckhoff.

Whenever someone from his home district came to visit, Dalén would ask for a description of home: the brownish-red slate road down to the village, lined with Swedish whitebeam, the ochre hue of the field stubble ... 'I owe you much thanks,' he would praise a skilled narrator. 'That's my home. I see it all. All of it.'

Dalén was often in the factory to receive foreign guests, and he still led research and development of products for the AGA brand: radio sets, gas welding equipment, spotlights for military motorcycles and optical aids. (An AGA laser reflector, used for distance measurement, was along for the first moon landing in 1969.)

In all, the company was granted 250 patents in Dalén's lifetime. He designed a delta-winged aeroplane, deemed to be 30 years before its time. He even built a car that ran on 16 horsepower with a top speed of 65 kilometres an hour; 8,000 were built in a German factory.

'Dalén sees better than we do,' a colleague said. 'We record laboratory reports on a Dictaphone and send the rolls to Dalén. They come back to us with his corrections, always concise and accurate.'

When Dalén was dying of colon cancer in 1937, it was his own invention – an apparatus for nitrous oxide anaesthesia – that eased his pain. He was active to the last, continually on the telephone, ordering new experiments and constructions. When he died on 8 December that year, he seemed frustrated that he had so much left to do.

It was conceived as Europe's first everyman car. AGA's German subsidiary launched the AGA-Car which won competitions in Russia but was never to be a successful seller. Gustaf Dalén appears to have been dubious about the new product. Afraid it might damage the company's good name, he wanted it to be called the Ega (acronym for ein gutes Auto – German for a good car). A total of 8,000 reached salesrooms. And only three have been found in Sweden. Another experiment was the AGA radio, another failure.

But his reputation was to live on.

Not least through the famous AGA cooker, today built in England and now weighing in at two tonnes. The price is approximately £10,000 and there is an 18-month waiting list.

Dalén reportedly dreamed up the idea on a train. (Where would Swedish inventors be without rail journeys?)

'Elma sweetheart, don't cast iron stoves waste wood?'

The result was a coke-fired oven with a pilot light and insulated hotplates. The latter proved to be a powerful argument when interviewing maids: the generous hotplate covers could be put to use drying wet infants. House cats were also fond of sleeping there. A point of special pride for the inventor was that the oven gave the blind some protection from accidental burns.

The world's first white kitchen oven reached the market in the nick of time. In 1929, AGA was floundering. The Great Depression in America was sending shockwaves across Europe. The employees at the Lidingö factory, previously loyal to a fault, were starting to grumble. But the AGA cooker ushered in a new heyday and renewed renown. The first orders came from the social elite: counts, barons and the fabulously wealthy Aga Khan, impressed that an oven could bear his name.

Stockholm's Post Office Museum still displays what is perhaps the oddest proof of the power of the AGA brand. In 1932, a Swiss gentleman, E. Gerber, who had apparently spotted the AGA cooker at a trade fair, decided to order one for his wife, directly from the factory. But how should he address his order? A few weeks later, a card was sent from Switzerland, postmarked Dobendorf, 7 January 1932, to the following address:

Luckan Skall Vera
Stängo
Schweden
[approximately: Door To Be Kept Closed, Sweden]

In the Thirties, the names AGA and Dalén were to become synonymous with internationalism, quality, expansion, ingenuity and taste.

When the farmer's boy from Stenstorp was finally laid to rest in Engelbrekt's Church in Stockholm on 17 December 1937, it was a

The Daléns' housekeeper cooking on her master's own homemade stove. The AGA stove is still being produced in England: a two-tonne version with a price tag of around £11,000.

statesman's funeral. The choir was decorated with pink begonias. Wreathes and flowers came from the student union at Chalmers Technological College, the Association of the Blind and the Danish Pilotage Authority. As the coffin was carried to the crematorium, torch-bearing AGA employees lined the road, lighting the winter's day with a necklace of beacons.

At a relayed message, ships across the world's sea-lanes lowered flags to half-mast.

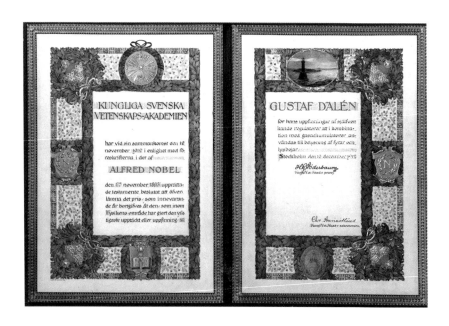

Condemned to die but satisfied. In 1937, Dalén was told he had colon cancer. The last pictures show a harmonious, constantly smiling man playing with the family dog by the fireplace. Gustaf Dalén was 68 years old.

The famous postcard from a Swiss customer who had misinterpreted the lettering on the front of the AGA stove. (What he took for an address was actually instructions on the stove's use.)

Gustaf Dalén was awarded the Nobel Prize on 10 December 1912, only three months after his accident in the quarry at Alby. Since Gustaf was still bedridden, his brother accepted the prize by proxy.

THE TELEPHONE KING

L M Ericsson 1846–1926

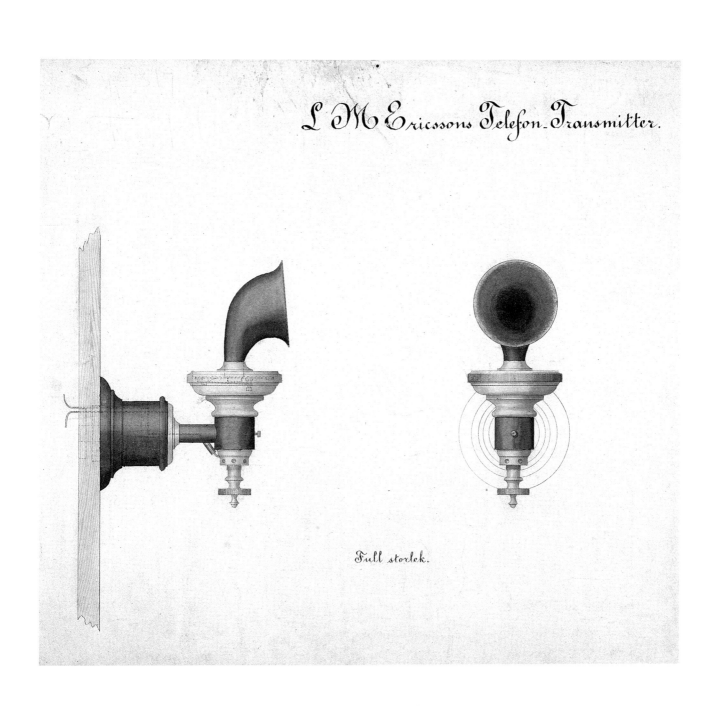

L M Ericssons Telefon-Transmitter.

Full storlek.

Two kilometres before reaching the spot, mobile phones lose coverage.

It is the backwoods. Tranquillity. A telephone-free zone.

Which is completely absurd, since telephony was possible in this part of Värmland province as early as 1863 – thirteen years before Alexander Graham Bell registered his famous patent!

In that year of grace, Sweden's first telephone line was rigged up, like a thin nerve, between a red dwelling in a forest clearing and a little smithy built of branches and peat down by the marsh. Its creator was a 17-year-old boy: a slightly underfed, shy kid who preferred his own company and who was to go through life speaking with a broad Värmland accent. They knew him locally as 'the saw-horse' because of his box-like build, a little hunched and sinewy. He looked strong but was knocked about as a farmhand and early on, began dreaming of a life devoid of lame plough-horses and rocks that seemed to spawn and multiply on the thin-soiled farmland.

But the boy had a steady hand. Put a school pencil between his sensitive fingers and he would swiftly sketch houses, machines and household utensils. Hand him a tin can and he would make his brothers and sisters a music box. Give him an engraving tool and he would make small, precise seals, almost works of art, that were to lead him all the way to the capital.

And lead him almost to depravation, too, since the boy could not keep from testing his skills on the Central Bank's sacrosanct currency. He and his friends were in the habit of spicing up their card games with fake coins punched out of tin scraps. Lars Magnus Ericsson took it a step further, imprinting the fake coins with currency emblems and giving them an authentic ring by adding pulverised glass to the molten tin. And since Ericsson was at best a mediocre card shark, the phoney money was soon in circulation in the community. The district police superintendent himself was handed one of the coins. It was not hard to guess who the counterfeiter was. The crime was a serious one, punishable by prison or whipping, but the superintendent perhaps realised that youthful energy was the true culprit. It was seen as little more than a schoolboy prank and there was no indictment. And no one could deny that the coins were beautifully done.

Evenings were gossip time in the village of Vegerbol and Lars Magnus grew steadily more frustrated. Stuck out here in the forest!

From underfed farm boy to wealthy telephony magnate. To mark his 80th birthday, Lars Magnus Ericsson (1846–1926) received the press at his estate near Tumba, just south of Stockholm. According to one newspaper, he had 'found a quiet retreat for his old age'. The life of this gifted man had been a continual back and forth between burning creativity and black melancholy.

Previous page: L.M. Ericsson's drawing of an 1880-model spiral microphone.

Wasting your life at the staid old Borgvik factory, where pay was 25 cents an hour and where they sniggered at his suggestions for improving the harrows and milk carts. Or transporting silver ingots by horse and cart, as his father did, from the mine up in the forest, for a meagre wage and little thanks.

Lars Magnus was happiest down in his smithy. There he was at peace, thinking and building. He wished he did not even have to go down to the village shop … wait a minute! He could communicate with the outside world through that string he had attached to the peat roof.

At home, they thought the idea was crazy. His mother, Maria, could never understand why it wasn't good enough to make a living from the soil, like all the family before him.

Speaking to someone through a thread? Lunatic ravings!

Well, it works if the thread is taut and attached to two cans. And Lars Magnus had already mastered that trick as a young lad. He had stretched ox bladder membrane – used by the poor to approximate window glass – like drum skin over a wooden pot. By scraping her fingernails across the slightly rough surface, his mother could signal that the potatoes boiling on the wooden stove were ready. It was a little wonder, she readily admitted.

Lars Magnus had read about a German schoolteacher called Johann Philipp Reis who had built something called a 'telefon'. It was like a telegraph, but emitted words rather than beeps.

I should be able to make one of those, Lars Magnus said to himself, with all the self-confidence of a 17-year-old.

'Just think, mamma, I could stretch a wire to the church so we could listen to the sermon from home!'

The story is probably apocryphal, since it has also been told about Samuel Morse and Guglielmo Marconi. But Lars Magnus was a gifted young man, evidenced already when as a twelve-year-old, he was able to show a mine captain a better way to pump water from a shaft.

The boy had once again disappeared to his smithy. Under the peat roof, he was constructing a strange gizmo with five components: a bladder retrieved from the most recent porky Christmas dinner, fastened to a metal plate, a pin, a wire charged with weak current and an electromagnet.

It was the first Swedish telephone, using the same basic principle for all telephony, up until the cellular revolution of the 1990s: the

Twenty-six-year-old Lars Magnus Ericsson, second from the left, with the other promising young talents awarded a state travel grant in 1872. They were shortly to leave for Switzerland, Germany and Russia.

A squat child, he was known as 'saw-horse'. But at 25, Lars Magnus Ericsson had a better physique and more poise but was still said to be quiet and somewhat meek.

The Ericsson homestead at Nordtomta, where 17-year-old Lars Magnus put together his first telephone, using a pig bladder and metal pins. Today, the farm is a museum to the region's famed son. The view is the same, although forest has encroached further on the farmland.

telephoner speaks at a membrane. The membrane vibrates, producing in turn vibrations in the pin. The movement is transported via a wire charged with weak current to another telephone, where another membrane is made to vibrate by another pin.

Simple but brilliant.

And astonishing that the concept could occur to someone way out in the deep forests of Swedish Värmland, far from institutes of learning and technical industries. By all accounts, Lars Magnus never completed more than five years of schooling in Vegerbol village. He learned to read and write, and little more. He was not even good enough for compulsory enlistment, rejected by the army as 'generally weak'. He was happiest when at his workbench. Later, in the autumn of his years, he wrote in a kind of testament to his son, Lalle: 'I was free to pursue my inclination for woodwork and sundry childish notions.'

That letter remains one of the few clues to the mystery of Lars Magnus Ericsson.

Lars Magnus Ericsson would always stick out with his total lack of higher education. He was a prodigy without papers as he trudged into Stockholm one day in 1866. His stubble was thick, his hands rough from work on the farm and a migratory existence as a mineworker, railroad builder and apprentice smith. All his jobs had been poorly paid, but in what free time he enjoyed he engraved and sold seals. And he also made a brief comeback as a counterfeiter – one story has it that he ran a trade in souvenir Norwegian bank notes while working on a rail gang.

The small capital he saved allowed him to take the plunge and move to Stockholm, which was almost as daring as emigrating to Minnesota or Illinois. A companion in the adventure, Carl Johan Wennberg, lost his nerve and turned back for home.

Getting a start was heavy going, even for a telephony king-in-waiting.

Factory owners peered sceptically at this rural apparition. 'No diploma? Sorry, young man, but we've got a lot of applicants. Come back when you've got an engineering degree.'

His saving was his seals. The Öller & Company Telegraph Factory was interested in seeing diplomas and certificates but all Lars Magnus could fish out of his pockets was his evening hobby work. It was well drawn and impressed the boss.

A telephone tycoon to be and his devoted wife. Hilda Ericsson was almost as enthusiastic about telephones as her husband. When still confined to bed after giving birth, Hilda wound wire on spools for her husband.

Ericsson's first telephone, based on an Alexander Graham Bell model left for repairs at Lars Magnus's workshop.

Could the young man also make company nameplates?

'Yes.'

'Good, make one for the company right away. If it is acceptable, you'll be given two kronor (approx. twenty cents) a week and a bunk in the workshop. Satisfactory?'

It was satisfactory. The engraver from Värmland would stay with Öller & Co. for six years. The company made telegraphy equipment and Lars Magnus hungrily absorbed all development findings. He became the company's eccentric and its star. When his workmates went out drinking, he saved his money, drinking milk and travelling fourth class on trains. In 1872, he trundled off to the Continent on a government travel grant and for three years worked in Germany, Switzerland and Russia. It must have been one of the Swedish government's best-ever investments. When Lars Magnus Ericsson returned, it was with a firmer posture and a sackful of ideas. He spoke fluent German, knew more about telegraphy than most people in Sweden and was ready to start his own company.

On the first of April 1876 he affixed a sign, 'Lars Magnus Ericsson's Workshop', to a top-floor door on Number 15, Drottninggatan street, in central Stockholm. It was a modest start for an industrial empire: the company's capital was all of 3,900 kronor (approx. $400), most of it from Ericsson's partner, Carl Johan Andersson, also from Öller. The nameplate hid a 13-square-metre kitchen, two foot-operated lathes, a set of tools and a twelve-year-old errand-boy. The company's first commission was to repair the police telegraph for a fee of two kronor. The next was to transform telegraphy symbols to letters, at the behest of the Swedish Railway Company director of telegraphy, J. Storkenfeldt.

Lars Magnus filled the order to the client's satisfaction and won a new one for twelve apparatuses. In the autumn of that year, 1876, he noticed a small newspaper article headlined: 'A Talking Telegraph'. A Mr Alexander Graham Bell in the United States had invented 'a miraculous machine that clearly and precisely transports uttered words from one end of a telegraph to the other'. It was in fact reminiscent of the old pig's bladder from Vegerbol. On 21 and 22 August 1877, Bell's invention was demonstrated in Stockholm for the first time, with Lars Magnus Ericsson in attendance. He saw that Bell had taken Reis's idea and refined it. And what he had created was undeniably impressive.

Ericsson's first real workshop, at Oxtorget square in Stockholm. This is where the new company set up shop when the family kitchen became too cramped. The first employee was a 12-year-old messenger boy.

By 1880, the L.M. Ericsson Company, now with all of nine employees, was expanding strongly and needed to move again. The new premises were on Biblioteksgatan street in Stockholm.

Telephone workers at the turn of the 20th century installing lines high above the roofs of the Swedish capital. Soon all of Sweden would be linked. The church in the background is Hedvig Eleonora.

A telephone station near Skanstull in Stockholm in the 1890s, when the Swedish capital had a population of 210,000 and had the highest telephone density of any city in the world. In 1895, Stockholm had 17,000 telephones. The windmill visible in the background is still standing.

Storkenfeldt of the Railway Company did not agree. He sniffed at 'a telegraph that cannot write'. What it lacked was ... dignity. The state Telegraph Department felt the same way and in an official letter to the government in k877 quoted the Latin adage: 'verba volant, scripta manent' (words fly, what is written remains).

Far less sensitive was a certain Henrik Tore Cedergren, son of a jewellery merchant. He proposed the installation of Sweden's first telephone line, connecting the family jewellery outlet and his own apartment, both on Drottninggatan street. He had a weak heart and was anxious to limit his walking.

Lars Magnus realised that Bell's telephone did not have a patent valid for Sweden, which meant that the invention could freely be copied. Lars Magnus easily worked out several small improvements, making the instrument less clumsy and voice reception clearer. Besides, Bell's telephones were prone to develop faults, which became obvious with a growing queue for repairs. That year, Lars Magnus learned a lot. By the end of 1878, he had sold his first telephones at 55 kronor (approx. $5) each, with an extra charge for cable, and had exchanged vows with 17-year-old Hilda Simonson, daughter of a saddle-maker to the Swedish royal court.

There is a lovely version of how they met: Lars Magnus was walking through Stockholm one day when he heard organ music from an open window. But the notes were flat. Since he had absolute pitch, he knocked on the door and offered to tune the instrument.

The organ turned out to be impossible to tune, but that did not stop the music. The girl who opened to his knock turned out to be more harmonious. She was in fact under-age, but a written appeal to the King, as custom demanded, produced both a dispensation and a lifelong marriage. Among her wedding presents was, fittingly, an organ built by her betrothed. That organ can be found today front row centre in the church at Värmskog. It has a four-octave range and still makes delightful music.

Probably closer to the truth is the version in which Lars Magnus met Hilda simply because the Royal Stables wanted a telephone installed. Either way, Hilda would be his 'sweetheart' for the rest of his life, his loyal helper, mother of his four children and the company's office manager. Their friends claimed that her greatest contribution was in tempering her melancholic husband. Lars Magnus had

'Stay on the line, please!' Ericsson soon developed a new way to build exchanges. To supplement exchanges manned by nimble-fingered operators, he created what was called a 'multiple board' that could handle ten lines automatically.

Jeweller Henrik Tore Cedergren was Sweden's first telephone subscriber; he needed a telephone line because of his bad heart.

Today Ericsson is a telecommunications giant with tens of thousands of employees in 140 countries. In 1889, the family was considerably smaller; besides the founder Lars Magnus himself, there were a number of quaint characters: 'Lasse the Louse' Larsson, 'Farmer boy Pelle' Pettersson (famous for getting his fingers caught in the milling machine) and Gabriel Bildsten, the messenger boy who was the first employee, now promoted to stockroom boss.

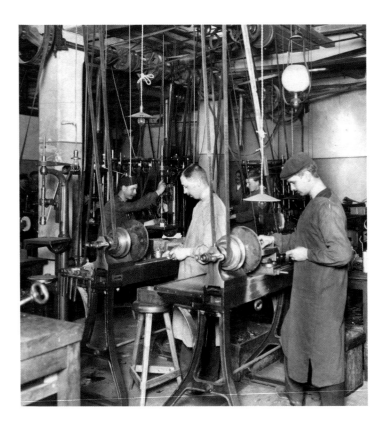

FABRIQUES DE TÉLÉPHONES DE LA SOCIÉTÉ L. M. ERICSSON & C.ᴵᴱ
A STOCKHOLM.

a dark side, exacerbated by the sudden death of their two-year-old son John in 1881. His sole spur was his creativity: idle, he reverted to dark pondering.

Hilda came from the yeomen of the agricultural heartland of Östergötland province and was, thankfully, the right stuff. There was nothing human or technical that could ruffle her. Not even four births could stop her assisting her husband: from her 'accouchement' bed, she wound spools for her husband's Drottninggatan workshop.

Which was now in rapid expansion.

By 1880, the workshop staff had increased to nine and the company moved to larger quarters. Manufacturing of telephones was now only part of the company's business operation. Stockholm had a telephone network set up that same year, but most people found the subscription charge too high. When the city of Gävle, north of Stockholm on the Baltic coast, called in the Bell Telephone Company, Bell wanted to set subscription charges at 200 kronor (approx. $20) per customer. A local industrialist asked Ericsson to put in a bid.

He did. Both for telephones and the infrastructure. And Ericsson's apparatus, in the opinion of three technical consultants, was 'better made, and had a better ringing instrument as well as a better-made microphone than Bell's, which also twisted'.

None of the telephones, however, had a range of more than 100 kilometres. At this stage, there were only single wires and the signal was dampened when returning through earth. You had to shout to be heard at a distance.

In Gävle, a local telephone company installed lines. In Stockholm and other towns, the National Telegraph Board provided that service. The Board purchased its first telephones from the Bell Company but quickly changed to the cheaper Swedish models. Ericsson's first foreign order came from Bergen, in Norway. The need for telephone exchanges soon became apparent, and even here, L.M. Ericsson turned to foreign patents. Encouraged by Henrik T. Cedergren, a forceful, unsentimental gentleman whose bushy moustache gave him the look of a Swedish Don Quixote, Ericsson developed a multiple board, an automatic exchange that could handle ten lines.

The Bell Company's price-setting system irritated Cedergren and prompted him to start his own telephone company, Stockholms'

'His master's voice' – a classic standard model from 1892, known as the Dachshund.

The heart of Swedish telephony: an interior from the Tulegatan street factory where L.M. Ericsson fine-tuned his approach – plagiarizing his competitors' best ideas but adding fresh improvements.

The telephony palace at Tulegatan street in Stockholm. A former business colleague, Henrik T. Cedergren, originally owned the factory but when Ericsson noticed his own orders drying up, he simply bought out his pesky rival.

Telephony director Lars Magnus Ericsson at 49. Through innovative design and cheap products, Ericsson founded an empire that would ultimately stretch across the world.

Allmänna Telefon AB, SAT, and enlist Lars Magnus Ericsson, situated a few doors away, as his main supplier.

In two years, Ericsson's staff grew from nine to 50 and the company was compelled to move to even more spacious digs on Tulegatan street. At the turn of the 20th century, there were 1,000 employees and the company was producing 50,000 telephones a year, mostly the popular 'dachshund' design, its four stocky legs ubiquitous in well-to-do Swedish homes.

In 1887, SAT built a large telegraph and telephone office on Malmskillnadsgatan street, with a 7,000-line capacity and Lars Magnus Ericsson as equipment supplier. The building's towers became a landmark and when incoming herring boats were sighted, a pennant would be flown from one of the towers for the entire city's notification.

The friendship between the two gentlemen cooled when Cedergren decided to start manufacturing his own telephones and switchboards. When the Telegraph Board did the same, Ericsson had suddenly lost his two biggest customers. Troubled, he toyed with the idea of closing down his Stockholm business and moving to St Petersburg, where the company already had a repair workshop.

History could well have taken an entirely different turn. Ericsson could have become ЭРИКССОН and disappeared from Sweden forever. But Lars Magnus clenched his teeth, checked his capital, and bought the SAT factory instead. It was a masterful move, but also his last as boss. In 1900, to everyone's surprise, the telephone king abdicated, selling all his shares. He was 54 years old and at the zenith of his career. There were no known schisms within the company board.

Perhaps he simply felt burnt out and used up.

Lars Magnus Ericsson had been a hard worker for 40 years. The most recent years had been a strain on his family and his health. Late nights had been spent on new solutions, and he fretted that his company had grown too large and become too vulnerable.

He was a man of simple beginnings, and might have felt inferior beside the company's young hotshots.

'Desk jockeys!' he muttered. Cedergren's self-confidence also made Ericsson feel socially second-rate. He was more at home on the factory floor. Ericsson's employees were paid better and had shorter hours than average. From 1891, employees enjoyed free medical benefits and funeral subsidies. Hilda was a pioneer for female labour.

Gender segregation in the first Ericsson factory. The men were engineers and designers; women wound wire onto spools and were paid far less.

His rough, Värmland accent and simple dress gave Ericsson an aura of honesty. He could be both gruff and morose, but this was mostly innate shyness. When Stockholm University later wanted to give him an honorary doctorate, he refused in a terse letter: 'As my conscience cannot ignore my limited qualifications for the honour, I am compelled, for inner peace, to decline.'

A copy of the letter was saved in an envelope inscribed: 'To be kept as a souvenir from 1 April 1909, and as proof of the lavishness of honorary distinctions at the time.' Even as a child, he had had difficulty in accepting praise. Now it had become almost an obsession to continually preach that 'man is a by-product, action the product'. Offered a seat on the city council, he again demurred.

In pictures from the turn of the century, he often appeared tired. His wife recalled that he could burst into tears behind the morning paper, from pure exhaustion. The idea took root of retiring from the hustle and bustle to the farm at Alby, south-west of Stockholm, that he had bought in 1895.

One of the stories Lars Magnus Ericsson most liked to tell was when, as a 20-year-old vagabond, he arrived at Alby farm and asked for a night's shelter. When they showed him the door, calling him a 'good-for-nothing vagrant', he vowed to return one day and buy the property.

He was unhappy as a young farm worker, but as a property owner with an Old Testament beard, he overflowed with energy and concern for his flock. He purchased the most modern agricultural machinery, installed electricity, and built a bell tower and a windmill as well as housing for the farmhands. One of his more daring experiments was to make an electric plough. It was a failure, but gave people in the district something to talk about for a long while.

A newspaper article spoke glowingly of his copper-roofed barn 'where the visitor – first requested to use the disinfectant pan at the door, intended for the shoes – finds not only curtains and fly-traps but also the unusual pleasure of fresh barn air, achieved through electrically operated ventilation fans'.

In 1906, he acquired neighbouring Hågelby gård farm and moved there for good in 1913. His creativity was still unceasing; it was in his blood. But now it was applied to magnificent constructions in painted cement: an echo temple, a lookout tower, an enclosure wall, a well pavilion and a washstand with eleven feet and a roof.

Paradoxically, the ageing L.M. Ericsson was increasingly a loner, preferring to write rather than talk about his invention. Only 54, he had abruptly walked away from his creation, selling all his shares and withdrawing to his estate to concentrate on testing his theories.

A model farm with electric ploughs, a revolutionary ventilation system, wind power, fly traps and shiny copper roofing. Alby farm in Fittja, close to Stockholm, was Ericsson's last great experiment. In 1913, he gave the farm to his favourite son Lalle, who was never happy as a farmer and died early. At Alby in September 1912, another Swedish inventor, Gustaf Dalén went blind in a controlled explosion that went wrong.

Hågelby also had a special building reserved for passing tramps. Lars Magnus had not forgotten his days as a 20-year-old.

Their home welcomed friends and guests, and once a week, Lars Magnus took Hilda to the opera. Theirs was a harmonious and loving marriage, according to most observers. But their son-in-law, Knut Harald Giertz, Anna Ericsson's husband, disagreed. In a family chronicle he wrote: 'The discord was perhaps not apparent to outsiders, but within the family there were long periods in which not a word was exchanged.'

In the chronicle, Lars Magnus was portrayed as a taciturn oppressor, demanding and slow to forgive. 'He never forgot words spoken with no other intention than to be of the moment. He hid them away, allowing them to grow monstrously in his imagination until the dam gates burst. And when he exploded, it was with all his intensity and all his violent energy.'

Lars Magnus reportedly had a sense of humour, but preferred to keep his mouth shut, and never gave speeches. If there was something he needed to say, he would write it down, after scrupulously polishing the phrases in his mind. The Telephone King would rather send a letter than speak into one of his telephones.

Among his children, it seemed that Anna best coped with her father's melancholy. She had inherited some of it. Father and daughter made several trips to the Continent, with her as his private secretary. She was conscientious and clever at languages, tapestry, flower arranging and mountaineering. After her father's death, she took over Hågelby gård and managed it until 1964.

Gustav, one of her two brothers, was the unhappiest. 'I will never properly grow up until Father has died,' he complained. 'Nothing on this Earth could make me be manager of the L.M. Ericsson Telephone Company. That would be the worst misery that could happen to me.' Gustav was a competent sculptor and made a bust of his father. He opened a car workshop and built a high-powered car known as The Snake, which became legendary in his Stockholm neighbourhood. 'Gifted, but wasteful,' was his father's judgement. He found his son too fond of parties. Lars Magnus himself was almost teetotal, only on occasion seen with a cognac snifter in his fist.

His relationship with his other son, Lars Magnus Jr or 'Lalle', was complex. Lalle was adored by his father but was deeply unhappy

It began with a scratchy noise over a wire between his mother's kitchen and the young Ericsson's workshop down the hill. A few decades later, L.M. Ericsson was famous and his company shares of great value to the kingdom. Advertising was varied and voluminous, even in the early days.

because of his inability to structure his life. His father's shadow was overbearing. While still 13, Lalle was receiving long letters from his father, often ending with ponderous exhortations: 'Should you wish to further reflect on destiny, remember that fear of God and an upright moral standing, in combination with dutiful work, are the greatest reward as life enters its autumn.'

Lalle was unhappy and awkward as the new squire of Alby. The stench of manure and the smell of horses bit hard on his sensitive lungs, despite his father's electric fans. There was a history of tuberculosis in the family and Lalle died in 1921, only 20 years old, to his father's unblemished sorrow.

The old titan's last years were heavy.

Looking back on his life, Lars Magnus saw mainly the dark parts. 'My first years were under the guidance of a good and respected father, but his sudden demise brought the first serious blow.' There is profound tragedy in his brief note that because Öller & Company received him so generously, for the first time in his life 'with deep gratitude, I looked upon life with a lighter heart than ever before, and experienced the first inkling of a joyful life.'

Lars Magnus retained his childhood Christian faith throughout his life. Late in life, it prompted studies in philosophy and religious brooding. In 1924, he was diagnosed with Parkinson's disease, making it impossible for him to hold a pen. The former seal engraver and counterfeiter could no longer write nor read. When death came two years later, it was almost a deliverance, in the form of a sudden cerebral haemorrhage.

He had never felt comfortable with middle-class ceremony, so his burial at Botkyrka, just south of Stockholm, was Spartan.

'Nameless I entered the world, nameless will I leave it,' he had said: one wonders how he would have reacted to his name becoming a global trademark, and that the company bearing that name has almost 60,000 employees in more than 140 countries.

A single adornment was permitted on the stoneless grave: a simple fir branch, brought from the edge of the forest at Ericsson's childhood home in Vegerbol.

But the story does not end there. If you play Trivial Pursuit, you discover that the correct answer to: 'Who invented the telephone?' is neither Lars Magnus Ericsson nor even Alexander Graham Bell, but

the German, Reis. In truth, a total of eight people could compete for the honour. The most fantastic claim is that Englishman Robert Hook had, in 1667, built a machine based on electro-magnetism that could 'talk across a considerable distance'.

Lars Magnus Ericsson was hardly first – and not even with the telephone exchange, as many maintain. He probably did not even have the idea of combining the loudspeaker and microphone in a handset. The accepted story is that a colleague, Anton Avén, linked the two parts with a sawn-off broom handle in 1884 so he could keep a hand free while testing wiring. A Frenchman had actually had the same idea five years earlier, but judged that handsets could be used only by telephone operators, not mere mortal subscribers.

So what did Lars Magnus Ericsson actually do?

The answer is that earlier than anyone else, he understood how to improve and exploit the new invention. He also had an unerring sense for design. Often, there would be a completed sketch on his bedside table when dawn broke. In the workshop, he would make quick chalk sketches in the morning and by evening a new prototype would be ready. He saw the finished product in his mind's eye even before it was drawn on paper.

At the time, Sweden was a poor country but was creating telephony products that astonished the world. The Värmland farm boy had a sharp nose for people's needs. In 1886, Stockholm was suddenly found to have the world's biggest telephone network with more than 4,800 subscribers. It was largely thanks to Lars Magnus Ericsson. His cheap products were exactly right for the price war that broke out in 1900 between Cedergren's SAT (which in 1888 had acquired a controlling interest in the Bell Company) and the Swedish Telegraph Board.

Heated competition squeezed prices and 15 years later, the Telegraph Board would emerge victorious to create a monopoly that, paradoxically, would benefit consumers. One system had triumphed: all local networks were under the same umbrella and all Swedes could call each other.

And all of them spoke into apparatuses that were derived from a Värmland pig bladder.

'Nameless I entered the world, nameless will I leave it.' At 82, Lars Magnus Ericsson died and was photographed on his deathbed by court photographer Bertil Norberg. The last years had been dismal; the great inventor had slipped into gloomy soul-searching and religious brooding. His dark view of life resembled Alfred Nobel's in many ways.

THE PERFECTIONIST

C E Johansson 1864–1943

t used to be said that only two people had the right to enter the great Henry Ford's office without knocking: his son Edsel and a former blacksmith, Carl Edvard Johansson of Eskilstuna, Sweden.

It is not certain whether the Swede ever used the privilege. If you're the world's most cautious man, you stick to convention. Quiet, shy and with an ear trumpet constantly clasped behind his back, the old man is said to have stood outside Ford's door until the correct time, at which he would knock, enter and dutifully present his latest research.

'Seven minutes late for work. Disgraceful. But the only time for three years,' he wrote in his diary for 18 December 1926 and despite the prim script, you can almost feel him quivering with indignation.

He had been on his way to the Ford factory in Detroit, and had got a puncture. For a man who made precision his vocation, to lose time in this way was tantamount to a defeat in battle.

Observing the man was 'like looking at one of his gauge blocks: square and stubby, like the chunks of steel he spends his time with', someone wrote, watching C.E. Johansson in his later years, waddling along the pavements in Eskilstuna on his way to his factory, his 80 years notwithstanding.

If Gustaf de Laval (the man who invented the separator) was the zany, absent-minded professor among Swedish inventors, C.E. Johansson was their stuffy pedant. Seldom has anyone so rigidly lived as he preached. And never had a brainstorm so accurately reflected its inventor's personality.

'I have always worked with a degree of care; I have never hurried and I've had one or two ideas that no one else had' was his own summation of his life and career. That same modesty and lack of pretension was present in his famous invention. Which was good, because the first impression was not striking: a few bits of steel in a wooden box, a chamois cloth for dusting, and the inventor himself, bashfully mounting the podium to demonstrate his 'miracle'. An ear trumpet poked out from his suit pocket: the man was half-deaf – the result of complications from a bout of influenza when he was 30 – rendering him reserved and slightly taciturn. His voice was a monotonous drone. He was, in a word, boring.

'It's a bluff, a chicanery!' exclaimed the respected Dr Benoit at the Académie des Sciences in Paris, on first hearing of Carl Edvard Johansson and his 'magic box'.

'The world's most cautious man', Carl Edvard Johansson (1864–1943) of Eskilstuna, demonstrates the famous gauge blocks that helped to accelerate mass production at the Ford Company and elsewhere. Without gauge blocks, no conveyor belt. The blocks were so perfectly polished that they seemed almost to stick together – you could hold all 102 straight out like a sword.

Previous page: C.E. Johansson's gauge blocks were a 'box of tricks' that no modern industrialist could do without. There were often 102 parts, or, as here, 46.

This was in the first years of the 20th century and the learned gentlemen holding in their hands the weights and measures of the world were seated around a massive table in Paris, sceptically fingering the polished pieces of metal with neat figures etched in by a sure Swedish hand.

The gathering resembled a moustache contest more than an international approvals committee. But then, C.E. Johansson was claiming he could slice a human hair into 200 parts and then measure the parts with his ingenious apparatus.

No wonder the Parisian gentlemen almost guffawed.

Although perhaps they were somewhat fascinated by the degree of smoothness of the metal pieces – smoother even than glass. When two pieces were held together, they would stick so tightly that none of the men could pull them apart. They had to be pressed apart, like rubbing the palms of two hands together. Put together in a row, they formed a rod so stable that it could be held out like a sword without falling into pieces. It was as though the atoms in the metal clung together.

Extraordinary, but obviously useless in the opinion of both Dr Benoit and the head of the Swedish Patent Office, which would stonewall Johansson for years because it found his invention 'not an industrial product'.

This was the initial reaction of the academic world. C.E. Johansson's block gauges or slip gauges must be sorted among the inventions that needed most time to break through. He was 30 when the idea came to him, but nearer 60 when he was finally given a job at Ford and could see his life's work change a global industry. Quietly and slowly, he had built his reputation, all the while helping the wheels of industry spin ever faster.

Moderation in all things was his greatest virtue. It was there even when he was a child. Sawmill worker Johan Johansson's Carl Edvard was a well-behaved boy, little interested in pranks. He would walk the ten kilometres to school every day from the family home in the stony fields southwest of Arboga, in south-central Sweden. Evenings would be spent in father's workshed, turning out rolling pins, matchboxes and butter trays for mother Carolina, or to sell cheaply to neighbours.

From his father the boy inherited care and accuracy but also a richly

As a young schoolboy, Carl Edvard kept a diary for his adventures. He also used his father's work shed to put together his earliest creations, using butter tubs and rolling pins.

Från havet steg vinden i lekande
logg, och sade till dimman giv rum
jag vill ogg. Han sade till klockan
i tornet hur sjön är dagen som ra-
ndas ring samman till bön.

Han svengde kring skeget och ropte
slå ut, du sjöman ditt segel ty nat-
ten är slut. Och han inåt landet
han gorde-ett slag, och manade bo-
nden stå upp det er dag.

Han sade till åkren de fattigas
hogg, nu buga dig gullax nu-sol som
går upp. Han minde på tuggen vid
gården i byn, upp härom och hals

inventive mind, attracting admiration even in a region and a time spoilt with cunning old farmers and survival artists.

Carl Edvard was born on 15 March 1864, six years after the introduction of the metric system in Sweden, and quickly indicated a strong need to measure, shape and control his environment.

At the age of eleven, he was already writing a diary; the entries are astonishing for their wealth of detail and for the boy's penmanship, if not for spelling. When 13, Carl Edvard would make tiny drawings of farmers on horseback and knights brandishing swords, with on the following page a note of the height of the cylinder for the steam engine he was building.

That machine has been preserved: it is a small masterpiece, with ornate legs and tastefully placed rivets. And it was merely a taste of what was to come. Together with his brother, Arvid, C.E. was soon experimenting with a 'horseless carriage with gear drive' and writing school 'esays' about 'Gunpowder' and 'Gold' interwoven with pious statements that might run on for an entire page. 'A child of God I am.'

There is a noticeable streak of Lutheranism, colourfast through life.

In old age, C.E. Johansson summed up his life as 'one long working day' and from the outset, he lived his life according to the motto: 'Work and Prayer'. His day usually began at seven and seldom ended before midnight. He did, to be sure, quit his first job, as an apprentice shoemaker, but not because of laziness. Instead, Carl Edvard dug out a small cave in a hillock on a farm to set up his own smithy. He was soon busy with orders from district farmers needing repairs on worn-out tools and machines.

Word spread fast about the capable young blacksmith, already doing work worthy of a master of the trade. And no short cuts, no rushed jobs. His squat body testified to a man with both feet firmly on the ground. He was mostly cheerful, seldom irritated and never drunk.

Renown was still in short supply when, 18 years old and seasick green, he stepped ashore in New York and was forced to spend his first night in the new land on a freezing floor in the company of thousands of other 'boat refugees'. Glowing letters from elder brother Arvid, now a foreman at a Colorado sawmill, had enticed C.E. over.

Two years later, the brothers travelled to St Peter, Minnesota to enrol at Gustavus Adolphus College. They studied technical subjects and mathematics and after school were captivated by roller-skating.

An early advertisement for Johansson's gauge blocks. Not even a strongman could separate the finely polished blocks. Yet it took time to convince industry of the need for Johansson's 'box of tricks'. He was reduced at one stage to borrowing money to help his company survive – and it tormented him.

In a letter home, Arvid attempted to describe the shoe as 'a kind of skate, equipped with four small castors running on axles embedded in gutta-percha'.

A footnote, perhaps. But also a snapshot of a family fascinated by innovations and technical gadgetry.

And all the time, C.E. Johansson was soaking up knowledge like a sponge. His college diploma was a filigreed document filled with testimonials and high grades. C.E. folded it carefully and packed it in his trunk. Home again in Sweden after three years' absence, C.E. unfolded the diploma shyly for his father's proud perusal.

He'd had enough of America, C.E. told people. There was little for him in a country where people were obsessed by money 'for money's sake'.

He held this opinion all his life.

And yet he returned to the United States 21 times. Sweden may have been a grateful stage for the magician from Eskilstuna — the man who more than anyone made 'Swedish quality' a concept with content — but the United States was first to give him recognition.

Recognition was not important in the beginning. Stubborn and single-minded, he sat locked in his room by his grinding wheel, polishing one masterpiece after another. When he finally packed his first gauges into a wooden box and ventured out to knock on doors, he was unsurprised to be treated virtually like a lunatic. He knew that what he had achieved was almost impossible. There has been endless discussion about whether C.E. Johansson really invented gauge blocks or whether he had merely improved an ancient idea. As early as the 18th century, there were 'Polhem screws' — a measurement device or template used in the manufacture of machines and weapons. Every self-respecting artisan owned such a device, allowing him to work without constantly having to use a measuring stick. Measuring rods were a sort of ready-reckoner for mechanics. When Johansson, then 21, was employed at the Beronius Mechanical Workshop in Eskilstuna, he had been allocated a set. But unlike his workmates, he was not happy with them. The rods were too crude and unreliable. In the United States, he had seen the genesis of mass production. But conveyor-belt production was unthinkable without exact gauging rods. What good would it be if a factory produced a screw that was exactly 2,000 millimetres thick if the other suppliers' screws measured 2,073?

Johansson as a promising student at the Eskilstuna Technical Sunday and Evening College, graduating class of 1888. The moustachioed future inventor is second from the right in the back row.

Years later, Henry Ford arranged a spectacular demonstration. Three of his cars, from different factories and of different colours, were taken apart and their parts mixed. The cars were then reassembled, using parts taken from the pile. At the end, there were three cars of decidedly motley colour parked in front of the spectators. They looked ridiculous – but they all worked as well as before.

But in 1894 that was still a vision. The father of the Swedish machine-gun and combine harvester, Helge Palmcrantz, had years earlier created Sweden's first factory for spare parts, but little had happened in the intervening years. C.E. Johansson, now all of 30 years old, took the train to Germany's famous Mauser factory in Oberndorf. The Swedish armed forces had placed a significantly large order and Johansson was part of a state-appointed delegation sent to study the superior German production processes.

But the Mauser Werke was like all other factories: there were calibration gauges scattered everywhere, many even made of wood. Johansson the perfectionist was flabbergasted by their sheer number – did they really need more than 1,000 calibration gauges for production? They shouldn't need more than … (he did a swift mental calculation) … 102, surely?

On the long journey home, he was quieter than usual. His pen flew over his notepad. Once home, he locked himself in. Glancing again at the notepad, he began slowly and methodically to machine-cut the first of the steel blocks that would astonish the world.

But how did Johansson do it?

More than a century later, we still do not know for sure. He was using a rough steel-grinding wheel attached to his wife's rebuilt sewing machine. And a little oil as polish. The produced items were dipped into a stove-top bath of exotic fluids, heated to 100 degrees Celsius, to 'age' the metal. All else is shrouded in mystery.

Referring to the measuring tool used to give his steel blocks a precision down to thousandths of a millimetre, Johansson once wrote that he used it only at home and then 'behind closed doors, and it is securely locked up whenever I go out'.

Once at a dinner party when Johansson found himself owing a favour to a fellow guest, the latter cunningly demanded: 'Tell me the secret of your gauge blocks!' 'Patience,' Johansson replied, 'Lots of patience.'

The sewing machine belonging to Johansson's wife Greta that was refitted to polish his measuring blocks to uncanny precision. The work was done secretively, behind locked doors.

In 1909, the C.E. Johansson Company opened its first workshop in a modest house in Eskilstuna, south-central Sweden. The building housed eight machines driven by a five-horsepower electric motor. In 1954, this historic site was pulled down to make way for an apartment block.

The Johansson family outside their home near Arboga. C.E.'s father, Johan, is seated in the middle with mother Carolina on his left. C.E., 35 at the time, is wearing the cap. To the right is C.E.'s wife Margareta with their daughter Elsa on her lap. Always precise, C.E. had written on the back of the photograph: '22 July 1899 4.15 o'clock in the afternoon.'

Kopieringsmaskinen

Kopieringsmaskinen användes förutom till kopiering af underbeslaget, hanen och slutstycket äfven till åtskilliga fräsningsoperationer, såsom fräsning af plattan och laxen för rekylklacken å pipan m.m.

Under kopieringen aflöses arbetsstycket utefter en bestämd linia, som efter kopieringens fullbordan utgör dess konturer och i form öfverensstämmer med konturerna på en med fixturen (i hvilken arbetsstycket fästes) fast förenad ledare (mönsterskifva).

Detta åstadkommes derigenom, att ledarestiftet a, (se den å följande sida afbildade kopieringsmaskinen) som tillika med spindeln b. är anbringad å den vertikala sliden c och med denna fast förenad med ständigt bibehållande af samma afstånd från spindeln, föres utefter nämnde ledare, hvarunder den i spindeln fästade fräsaren bearbetar arbetsstycket utefter en linia, som öfverensstämmer med ledarens konturer.

Bordet d, å hvilket fixturen c är anbringad, kan medelst vefverf samt flera med hvarandra förenade kuggdref, af hvilka tvänne, g och h, ingripa i kuggarne på de å undre sidan af bordet anbringade kuggstängerna i, i', föras fram och tillbaka.

Samtidigt med bordet kan äfven den större, horisontala sliden j gifvas en emot detta vinkelrät rörelse medels vefven k och kuggdrefven l, l', af hvilka det senare

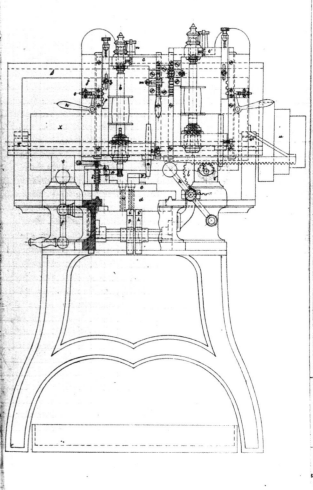

Behind locked factory doors in Eskilstuna, a world revolution in miniature was taking shaping without anyone suspecting. Certainly not his employees; they cut, ground and polished his magic rods, little suspecting that they were laying the grounds for the industrial superstructure of a dawning century.

Johansson's wife was also involved. The most cautious man in the universe had naturally been careful in his choice of spouse. When only 15, he had come across a newspaper article on a young man's choice of partner. He had cut out and saved a quote: 'Marry for love and get a wife; marry for money and get a boss; marry for position and get an accessory. Your wife will love you, your boss perhaps respect you and your accessory will merely tolerate you.'

Fredrika Margareta Andersson was, without question, a wife. Seven years his junior, she was the daughter of a brickworks foreman and the most loyal of spouses. Throughout her marriage, she was his backup and ground service, uncomplaining when her husband turned their home into a workshop. 'Standing by me, you seem so happy,' he once wrote in a letter. 'You hold me firmly by the arm and encourage me.'

Theirs seemed a happy union, although we have only his words to go by; his the only version preserved for posterity. In photographs, Greta Johansson is always in the background, constantly smiling and often with a daring new hat to go with her otherwise conventional attire. As well as bringing up their children – Signe, Elsa, Gertrud and Edvard – she also assumed responsibility for the chemical bath over the wood-fired stove. She was in charge of tempering the first steel measuring blocks in a kitchen pot.

In business, C.E. Johansson was just what you would expect: cautious and thrifty almost to the point of being frugal. 'I once borrowed 500 kronor from the bank and it was a bitter experience,' he remarked at the end of his life. His partner Arthur Spångberg was the driving force in their business. Spångberg worked hard to convince his careful friend of the need to invest and build new facilities. His pleas were sometimes met with home-made aphorisms such as: 'Better to reach shore in a small boat than to shipwreck on an ocean liner.'

More often, Johansson would simply lower his ear trumpet, indicating that the discussion was over. 'My peace pipe,' he called it. He was not one for divisive quarrels, nor one for imaginative planning.

He was a marvel of precision, even at his desk. This is an early copying machine from one of Johansson's sketchbooks.

In 1901, the C.E. Johansson Company was founded, but had to wait eight years for its own premises and another nine until the first subsidiary, in the United States, was opened. No leaping before looking, in other words. Slowly, deliberately, Johansson was fine-tuning his invention. Like a snail on a mission, he would add successive thousandths of a millimetre to his precision instrument.

He was brave and wary at the same time.

From the outset, Johansson seemed to realise he was sitting on a fortune, but was willing to bide his time. The world was not ready to understand and must be given time.

The occasional set of gauge blocks was sold to a forward-looking manager, but as late as 1911, the inventor himself was still travelling around Sweden on rattling provincial trains, trying to close orders in the southern provinces of Småland and Skåne.

The Royal Swedish Patent Office had been sceptical from the beginning, and Johansson's writings on the subject from the turn of the 20th century are a study in patience and quiet frustration: 'Patent not yet finally approved,' he wrote in his diary on 4 December 1898. A year later, in a letter to a friend, he mentioned that his application had been rejected yet again: 'I intensified work on my models so I could travel to Stockholm and, model in hand, prove they were in error.'

The fight to have a patent approved figured largely in his letters until it finally came in 1904 and was assigned Number 17017. The English had been far more accommodating: his patent had already been approved in London in 1902, and thanks to the advocacy of an engineer friend, Ternström, had been awarded a silver medal at the 1903 Paris World Exhibition – in the city where only a few years previously he had been rejected by Dr Benoit & Co. These same moustachioed gentlemen had changed opinion diametrically and from then on would be firm fans. Similarly, when a German manufacturer wrote a complaining letter, charging that Johansson's block gauges did not match a calibration device imported from France at the heady price of 10,000 francs, the next letter begged forgiveness for this hasty allegation.

Johansson's letters offer both light and demanding reading. Light, since his handwriting glides across the pages in even, leisurely flow – all preserved in carbon-copy in neat blue notebooks.

The American press was rapturous over Johansson's visit in 1919. The Swede was seen as having contributed to the Allies' victory in the First World War. Johansson was sceptical about the consumer society and its "insatiable craving for money".

The extraordinary Mr. Johansson from Sweden was in town to demonstrate his invention, capable of measuring a human hair split into 200 parts. His US lecture tour was a huge success.

=====: NOTICE :=====
...Technical Lecture...
ILLUSTRATED
Will be Given at the Club--on--Saturday Evening, November 22d, 1919
AT EIGHT O'CLOCK
By MR. CARL EDWARD JOHANSSON
Noted Swedish Scientist and Inventor of the
JOHANSSON GAUGES

This Lecture will no doubt be of very great interest to the mechanical men of our Club and our city

:: DON'T MISS IT

Also Under the Auspices of the Club, a Motion Picture Production Limited

THE TWIST DRILL
ITS USES AND ABUSES

Very truly yours,
MACHINERY CLUB OF CHICAGO
Entertainment Committee

THE DAYTON DAILY NEWS

FRIDAY, NOVEMBER 7, 1919

"The Millionth of an Inch"

Carl E. Johansson, the Swedish scientist, the man who first furnished the mechanical world with gauges giving accurate measurements to the ten-thousandth part of an inch and who later produced gauges divided to hundred thousandths and to the millionths of an inch, is visiting the principal manufacturing centers of America.

Mr. Johansson has been in Dayton since Thursday meeting the men of this city interested in precision tool work, the subjects of interchangeable manu-facturing, the limit system of production, etc.

A demonstration of some new types of precision tools will be made by Mr. Johansson in connection with a talk Saturday evening. He will have with him the only set of gauges ever made in millionths of an inch. The meeting will be held in the Auditorium of the Engineers Club at 8 o'clock. Admission free.

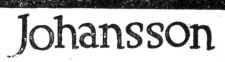

Johansson

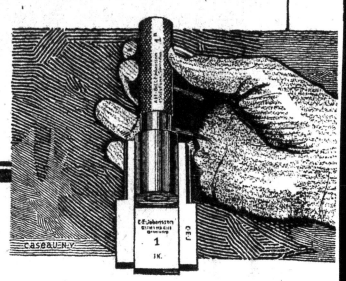

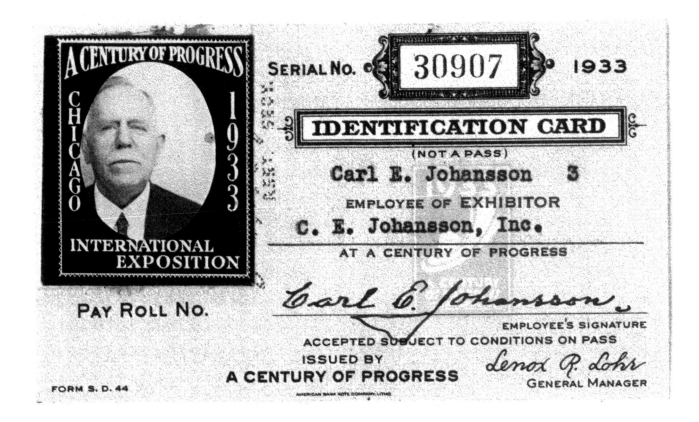

Demanding, in its dry detail and occasionally vexing need to give thoughtful though wordy advice to the world at large.

A two-page letter to his parents dated 15 December 1898 is almost entirely taken up with instructions for travelling the few dozen kilometres from their home to his, for the Christmas celebrations. There are meticulous, minute recommendations for how mother should keep warm. He recommends a covered carriage; offers to send over a heated sandbag for her feet and a fur with a collar that mother mustn't forget to turn up. It seems more like a mother's advice to her son than the opposite. In letters to his parents while he was still in the armaments industry, Johansson often included endless detail on the factory: working hours, prices, rates, cylinder measurements and so on. And his feisty father was quick to take note and reply: 'It is as if the Russians were hiding behind the next hill ready to advance, to judge by your haste to produce those muskets.'

Johansson's letter writing increased after the damage to his hearing in 1896. Perhaps his disability embarrassed him; perhaps it helped him focus more exclusively on work, making him even more fastidious.

Oddly, he could hear better in workshop noise than in a quiet parlour. All his life, he appeared 'mal placé' under the glow of chandeliers, seldom smiling. Outdoors, his hat hid the shyness in his eyes; a man on temporary leave to the outside world. It was as though he were not properly dressed without his factory apron and his cutting machine.

Witnesses remember that Johansson's favourite place was alone at work at the dining table, ordering his papers and noting memorable events in his diary: 'I intended to borrow a velocipede and pedal from Arboga to [his parents' home in] Lunger and back yesterday, but it appears difficult to find such a thing.

'I extend my thanks for the potato delivery.

'In the morning, Henning Pettersson and I were out exercising on one of the hillsides of Djurgården Park. In the afternoon, G.P. and I made our way to Hellby to call on J. Björnsson, who has commenced a bathing regime at the aforementioned spa. It was enjoyable in the woods, freshening and invigorating.'

The big breakthrough finally came, initially with his visit to the United States in 1919 and then with his acceptance as Henry Ford's confidant in Dearborn, Michigan in 1923.

By combining different measuring blocks, you could attain a precision of two thousandths of a millimetre. At the Ford factory in Detroit, C.E. Johansson showed how to find the exact measurement for one inch by combining blocks of 24mm and 0.4mm.

Carl Edvard Johansson's identity card, issued for the 1933 Chicago World Fair. Even at the age of 79, the old inventor would not stop travelling or learning.

Henry Ford kept two objects on exhibit in the lobby of his head office: the 'Encyclopedia Britannica' and C.E. Johansson's gauge blocks. For Henry Ford, they set the standards the world lived by.

Johansson looks slightly lost in pictures from 1919. When he left Sweden to inspect his factory in Poughkeepsie, New York, he was an anonymous 55-year-old. But on arrival, the American press was out in force, headlining his visit. He was hailed as one of the heroes who had won the war for the United States. The man himself was dubbed 'the world's most accurate man' and his life-story 'a twentieth century romance'.

Americans love inventors and self-made men. In the newspapers, pictures of Johansson's gauge blocks were captioned 'Johnny Blocks' or 'Johansson gauges' and the text advised: 'He will make one of these for you for 10,000 dollars.' Much was made of Johansson's visit to Thomas Alva Edison in the latter's laboratory. It is said that Edison chortled, 'Oh, so you're deaf too!' and nodded in approval when Johansson refused to reveal anything about his invention: 'Won't tell, eh? Well, he's all right.'

Johansson was invited to give a lecture in Daytona, Florida where he was welcomed with the words: 'Your gauges are wonderful!' In an opening address, Johansson's host, John N. Patterson, mentioned that he had been in Sweden himself 'to discover why they had so many great inventors'. Patterson had insisted on visiting a traditional old home and had been struck by the amount of clever detail and that everything was in wood: walls, roof, doors, nails, hinges, even locks.

'It's due to the harsh climate,' explained Patterson. 'The Swedes have become inventors because they were forced. They would not otherwise have survived.'

There may well be some truth in this. Certainly, C.E. Johansson's triumphant tour of America greatly helped Swedish industry's reputation abroad. 'The problem with this country is that everyone wants to make big things, and not bother with refining details,' wrote an American journalist, concluding wittily: 'The only immeasurable thing today is Mr Johansson's importance for mechanical engineering.'

There is a story about a Swedish engineer applying for a job with Henry Ford. When rejected by the great man and shown the door, the Swede blurted out that he was travelling with a great inventor, C.E. Johansson.

'C.E. Johansson? The C.E. Johansson? Send him in – he's got a job!'
'But how about me?' stammered the engineer.
'All right, you've got a job too. As long as you get Johansson!'

In 1932, C.E. Johansson returned to Gustavus Adolphus College, Minnesota, where he had studied as a 20-year-old. This time, it was for an honorary doctorate.

Johansson worked for 13 years for Henry Ford. It is difficult to guess how he felt about this 'promotion'. 'Once more, I find myself in another's employ, testing again what it is to serve others,' he wrote on 18 November 1923. 'But Mr Ford is a splendid man and leaves me to make my own decisions.'

Perhaps Johansson suspected that, at the age of 59, he was on the payroll more for his image value than anything else. The head office entry displayed a glass class with the 'Encyclopaedia Britannica' and Johansson's gauge blocks. 'Because what those books are for education,' Ford pronounced, 'the gauge blocks are to industry.' Yet it took more than three years for Ford to organise a proper workshop for Johansson to replace a temporary premises in an old flourmill that the Swede quietly called 'the treadmill'. As an inventor, he accomplished little or nothing in this period. Henry Ford was always jovial when they conferred and Johansson had been given the unusual right to enter Ford's office without knocking, and certainly, Johansson was on an enormous salary, but there was still a gnawing doubt.

'Obviously, I want to go on working as long as circumstances and my strength permit,' he wrote. 'But I am beginning to feel that there are limits.'

In July 1936, Johansson moved back to Sweden and Eskilstuna for good. He was 72, and humanly, should have been ready to put his feet up. Instead, he could be spotted every morning, shuffling along the pavement towards his factory. Always punctual. Always afraid of idleness.

When he finally died in 1943, he was an honoured citizen, a distinguished son of Eskilstuna, praised in obituaries for his modest nature, his donations to hospitals and churches and his abstemious character. His sole pleasure, apart from family life and his diary, was riding his motorboat up and down the 20-kilometre-long Näshultasjö Lake. In pictures, the water was always duck-pond calm: to the end, C.E. Johansson was a man who detested adventure and hated surprises.

But a storm would arise, all of seven years after his death.

When the Swedish-American sculptor Carl Milles created his renowned 'God's Hand' in 1950, it was partly in homage to C.E. Johansson. Milles saw in the master of the gauge blocks a creative force that gave the world structure and meaning through his bag of tricks. But when the City of Eskilstuna attempted to raise money from

The only place he would relax and let his hair down was on Näshultasjö Lake. His motorboat was one of the very few distractions and extravagances the extremely Lutheran Johansson allowed himself. He once summed up his life as 'one long day's work'.

One of the few private, slightly relaxed pictures of the always so well-tailored, tranquil C.E. Johansson and his hat-loving wife Greta. It was in Greta's kitchen the first gauge blocks were cooked up.

C.E. Johansson was honoured with a bust by prominent Swedish sculptor Carl Eldh. For much of his life, Johansson suffered from reduced hearing caused by a severe case of influenza. He was happier in noisy factories than in limelight.

local companies to purchase the sculpture, the managing director of the city's rubber stamp factory, A. Edvard Olson, announced he could no longer remain silent. In his eyes, Johansson was a fraudster. It would be more fitting, said Olson, to speak of The Devil's Hand, rather than God's. Because the true inventor of block gauges was Olson's partner, Hjalmar Ellström. 'It is my moral duty to prevent a statue being erected to the wrong man.'

Thus began the so-called Measurement War.

Modern reference books credit C.E. Johansson alone with the invention of the gauge block, but in the 1950s, small cracks appeared in the figurative monument to the world's most scrupulous man.

Briefly, the claim was that on his deathbed, Ellström had asked Olson to fight his cause. Ellström claimed that he had invented the gauge block in 1895, a year before Johansson, while both were employed at the weapons factory in Eskilstuna.

At first, Olson was dismissed as a grudging sensation-seeker, but when the chief biographer of the distinguished 'Nordisk Familjebok' encyclopaedia, Alvar Lenning, came out in support of Olson, all hell broke loose and a number of witnesses stepped forward:

- A grinder's assistant by the name of Andersson claimed to have seen a spyhole Johansson used to observe Ellström.
- In 1918 or 1919, it was alleged, Johansson ordered persons in his employ to enter Ellström's office and make drawings of the apparatuses he used.
- The daughter of another colleague, C.D. Hellström, said her father became upset when he heard that Johansson intended to show Henry Ford a 'hole indicator' device, 'since he [Johansson] did not seem to have the vaguest idea of how to use the instrument, but was counting on finding someone to help him'.

Lenning charged that Johansson could take liberties because Ellström was 'a happy-go-lucky chap who did not give a thought for tomorrow. Johansson would often come crying, begging for forgiveness or for economic favours, and Ellström would always weaken.'

In 1954, Lenning published his thoughts in a book, 'The Inventor of the Combination Block Gauge'. C.E. Johansson was described as 'indelibly cunning'; he 'never surprised anyone with his quickness of wit, had no hobbies, never tasted alcohol and had no interest in

Hardly a man of swift movement or fierce facial expressions. Through life, C.E. Johansson lived as he taught. A moderate man in every respect.

people other than his immediate family and those who belonged to his religious faith'.

Among those who rose to C.E. Johansson's defence – and they outnumbered the attackers – was his old partner, Arthur Spångberg. Spångberg said he thought the dispute had arisen because Ellström 'had not been compensated for some joining pieces he claimed to have originated'. Spångberg also raised the issue of the gauge blocks not being a new invention. They were in essence no more complicated than the combination of weights that accompanies every set of scales. The added value was in the unbelievable precision and the ability to understand the inherent potential. This was the essence of C.E. Johansson's genius. Hjalmar Ellström presumably did have an idea for gauge blocks as early as 1895, but lacked the strength, interest or ability to develop it.

Or was C.E. Johansson a bluff, a sleight-of-hand expert who spent a lifetime duping people – including the French Académie des Sciences and the world's greatest car-maker? Is it really The Devil's Hand and not God's that still stands before Eskilstuna City Hall?

The conclusion must be that the world's most pedantic man has gone down in history in a way he would have hated: with the nagging feeling that something was not quite right. All his life, he despised words like 'about', 'perhaps' and 'possibly'. A half-century later, these are words that stick.

The other uncertainty about C.E. Johansson was the mystery concerning his height.

His passports – and he wore out a good number – agree about the chestnut hair, the blue-grey eyes and the 81 kilos. But regarding the number of centimetres over ground level, there is a descending scale:

In 1916, he was noted as 174 centimetres tall.

In 1919, 1922 and 1923 he was 172 centimetres.

In 1931, just 170.

Presumably, 'old Johansson' became bowed with the years.

Still, it's strange when you realise that the only item that did not measure right in Carl Edvard Johansson's life turned out to be him.

It took years, but in the autumn of his life, Carl Edvard Johansson, former blacksmith, would become a celebrity. 'Husmodern' magazine honoured him in 1943 with a cover picture together with his grandson. 'My secret? Patience, lots of patience.'

Johansson's passport reveals that even the most exact man in the world did not always measure up: this particular year, 1916, he measured 174 centimetres.

MR WRENCH

J. P. Johansson 1853–1943

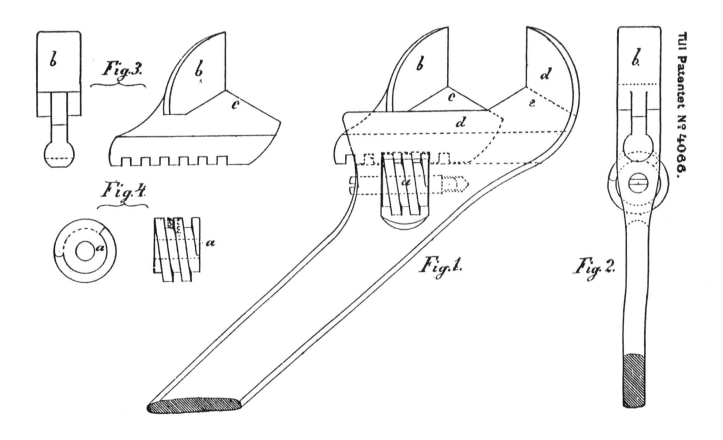

When Salomon August Andrée was packing supplies and equipment on the morning of 11 July 1897 before setting off on his ill-fated balloon voyage to the North Pole, one of the items he put into the gondola was a shiny wrench, or adjustable spanner, made of brass.

It was a present from his friend J.P. Johansson, a manufacturer from the city of Enköping, some 80 kilometres west of Stockholm.

The monkey wrench had been specially forged in metal that would not disturb sensitive compass needles. The wrench remained on board throughout the balloon's meandering journey, even though expedition members were constantly dumping item after item into the snow to retain height.

It is hard to imagine what you would use a wrench for at the North Pole. Perhaps for the sleds, or for repairing the cooking equipment. Andrée refused to discuss it. If you had a wrench, it was his firm conviction, you didn't need other tools. Johansson was a man to Andrée's taste and at the same time an opposite: earthy, reliable and feet firmly planted in his workshop. Swedes say, 'old love never rusts'; neither would tools wrought in brass.

How had this odd friendship come about?

In 1929, one year before a Norwegian expedition came across Andrée's remains on a small island off Svalbard, in the Arctic Sea, 56-year-old Johan Petter Johansson gave one of his rare interviews. Talking to the 'Vestmanlands Läns Tidning', he looked back on life, from being a shepherd boy to world fame as the Tool King of Enköping. As he recalled how he started out selling wooden rifles to school friends, he took the opportunity to chastise youth for their current indifference to the joy of work, opting instead for unproductive games: 'Sport has taken a strong upper hand, and more attention is given a good kicker than to a skilful fitter and turner.'

Out of the blue, Andrée's name came up. The two had met at the Swedish Inventors' Society; Andrée was the founder and Johansson a charter member. As well, Andrée was head of the Patent Office on nine of the occasions Johansson had applied for new inventions. All nine requests were endorsed.

The two men were like compass needle and magnetic pole: one anchored, the other spinning off and away. But there was mutual attraction; each fascinated by the other's expertise and eccentricity.

He was almost as resilient as his own pliers. Former shepherd boy Johan Petter Johansson (1853–1943) in action in his workshop, 84 years old. The man who gave us the adjustable spanner, or wrench, was a modest, self-assured smallholder's son whose start in business life was selling wooden rifles to schoolmates.

Previous page and below: J.P. Johansson's revolutionary adjustable wrench, patented 11 May 1892. Before the end of the next century, 100 million were produced. Astonishingly little change has been needed in the design.

'Don't go to the North Pole,' said Johansson, Andrée's senior by one year. 'Too dangerous.' And, prophetically: 'You'll freeze to death up there.'

But Andrée went.

'He was helplessly enthralled by the challenge,' remembered J.P. Johansson. 'He went. He had with him several of my tools, made in brass so as not to disturb the compass. They were swallowed by the polar sea, like the bold man himself.'

Johansson, in contrast, was a prosaic man. He was the only one of his family to remain in the country of his birth. Four brothers and sisters and both parents had steamed off for America on 14 April 1883 aboard the 'Albert Ehrensvärd', settling in Minnesota. When his widowed mother turned 86, her son made the only long journey of his life to see her.

'To thank her for what she had given me, not least in terms of my inherited talent for mechanical work. She had a good grip on the laws of nature, and did a lot of heavy mechanical work, and more intricate things too.'

The reporter asked Johansson if he had found anything new in America.

'Nothing to suit us. I had an enjoyable journey through the United States and Canada and saw many factories, but couldn't find anything new in the way of tools or suchlike that was unknown in Sweden. It is just that everything was on such an incredibly larger scale.'

Here is J.P. Johansson in a nutshell: in one of the pictures illustrating the article, he was out behind the house digging up worms for his chickens, clad in a suit and hat. His body was a farmer's: square and muscular. All his life, he had stood with his boots planted in the rich earth of Enköping. That his tools were world-famous changed nothing. There he was, his boots in the mud, unassumingly chatting, saying that the most important thing was that children get a good education. He had himself founded several evening schools and served on the local school board. His horizons may have been somewhat limited, but it made him a powerful realist. His 76 years notwithstanding, he dashed like a short bolt of grey lightning between the workshop's drop hammers and punching machines. 'The Director is at home everywhere and with everything,' gushed the reporter. 'As chummy with the machines as he is with the workers; he knows all

The residence known locally as 'Fanna Castle'. Johansson had a cellar workshop for experiments. In the foreground: Johansson's daughters, Tyra, Judith and Ingrid.

An earthy industrialist. Seventy-six-year-old J.P. Johansson digging for worms for his chickens, while his inventions were conquering the world.

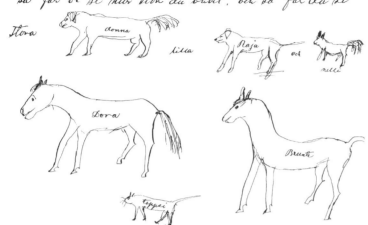

till Morfars lilla Inger.

Du skall vara snäll och komma och hälsa på oss snart
så får vi se hur stor du blivit, och så får du se

of them by name. He greets and is greeted, stopping to chat with a good word here and a friendly pat on the back there.'

This was an old-time patriarch in action. Everyone had long established their place in the hierarchy. Ties of trust – and not least of dependency – were strong between boss and workers in that small town. J.P. Johansson built their accommodation and lent them money. He held frequent parties for employees at his residence beside the factory, surrounded by stately oak trees and right where the ancient agricultural plain starts to spread out.

Johansson's benevolence towards his employees was renowned. It may have been because of the man's own origins. He strutted like a despot between the heavy tables and chairs of his home and its gilded mirror from a royal castle. The hallway was large and round, filled with contemporary wonders, with a radio in pride of place, the main status symbol. But he always emphasised his humble origins in a home dependent on contract labour. J.P. took pains never to appear self-important or overbearing.

'Our home was poor but happy. When I went to school, we used to practise with wooden rifles, so I made some to sell to the other boys – it was my first business!'

He was born on 12 December 1853. Thirteen years old, he attracted notice when he rebuilt his father's threshing-mill.

'He had a hand thresher which was heavy for us to pull and I thought the horse could help. So I made a guide wheel, put it upside down and put the axle in a drum under the carriageway. So the horse pulled the thresher along.'

It was a typical J.P. invention. Confronted with an everyday problem, he solved it. Everything had a commonplace, practical application.

'These kerosene lamps are so dangerous,' said his mother one day. 'If you youngsters ever break the glass, you'll burn the cottage down!'

'They should be made out of metal instead,' commented the young Johan Petter and trotted off to the tinsmith with a cartload of tins he had found, to learn how to solder.

'Father, you'll make the sugar dirty!' complained J.P.'s daughter when her father, straight from the factory, sat down to afternoon coffee.

'Then I'll have to invent a sugar-tongs,' answered her father, and straight after his coffee break sat down to design an implement that quickly become a fixture in Swedish households.

J.P. Johansson's letters and notes indicate a man of quiet humour, impressive inventiveness and a certain weakness for drawing. This letter to his daughter Inger shows that his pen was used for more than inventions.

The timid inventor receives guests in his imposing home at Fannalund. He preferred to be known as 'factory-owner Johansson' and talked readily about his poor beginnings in a tiny country cottage. The chandelier is a far cry from his mother's simple kerosene lamps that he always had to fix until he invented a replacement.

When still a youth and wanting to know the time of day, he made his own pocket sundial, with a fold-up indicator. When, as a 66-year-old, his eyesight was growing dim, he invented the pivot-necked Triplex Lamp to shine light on every close corner. He had already calculated that his employees' work would improve so radically that his investment would be repaid in six months.

And when in 1888 he created the first of his world sensations, it was mostly because the workshop's tongs were always missing when they were needed.

The pipe wrench was born of irritation. (Some authorities credit American Solymon Merrick with inventing the pipe wrench, or crocodile spanner, in 1835. Others say Merrick's tool was essentially a prototype for J.P. Johansson's.) Whenever there was an external job to be done, the mechanic would have to tote with him a cartload of tongs of different dimensions. 'Unnecessary,' reasoned J.P. 'Why not a single, adjustable wrench?'

It was the same story with the monkey wrench, or adjustable spanner, born as a logical little brother four years later. But all his life, he would love to pose for pictures holding the original pipe wrench, his darling baby. The monkey wrench would be along for the ride, peeping out of a coat pocket. In the press photographs, all that revealed the passing of the years was the progressive greying of his hair. The basic form of his tools was consistent. The fascinating thing about J.P. Johansson's inventions is that they were close to their final form from the very beginning. Once he had solved the moveable jaw problem, the monkey wrench sustained its shape for more than a century; the only real adjustment was having its shape 'prettified a tad', as the maker himself put it.

There is much to be learned in the progress of the shepherd boy to an accomplished worker of heavy metal. The farmer's cottage had quickly become crowded for the eldest of six brothers and sisters. And it was the golden age of the locomotive. On 18 January 1878, when all of 19 years old, J.P. disembarked from a steamship in Motala, an industrial port on Lake Vättern, Sweden's second largest lake. He was carrying 'a sack of clothes and one-and-a-half kronor, all that I had and all that I owned'. Norwegians were doing the gravel-laying work on the new line between Hallsberg and Mjölby, two south-central hubs and 'the Lapp boy' from further north, straight from peat-cutting

'Mr. Wrench'. This is the most published picture of Johan Petter Johansson, who loved to pose with his favourite tool, the pipe wrench. The monkey wrench or spanner did not provide as spectacular a picture. It would simply peek out of a vest pocket.

at home, became their gofer. In the autumn, he found himself in a town called Långängskrogen, boarding with the Ytterholm family in a house 700 metres from the railway line. The family's breadwinner was a part-time soldier. Mrs Ytterholm was fond of the teenager and looked after him. In return, he helped out by doing small repairs: kitchen utensils, a loom spool, a lock. The soldier's cottage is still there, and the current owners once found a railway worker's hat in the attic.

The Ytterholms' son, Johan Erik, was a musical instrument maker in Stockholm, and when he saw J.P.'s clever repairs, he exclaimed: 'You don't belong here – you're a mechanic. Go to the Munktell Company in Eskilstuna. I'll write you a recommendation.'

In fact, J.P. had to make about ten visits before the company's master mechanic, Lutman, took the youngster under his wing. 'You're a stubborn fellow!' he sighed, sending him off to hold down rivets in the steam boilers – 'a dumb and noisy job'.

The Munktell factory was obviously not a final destination. Factories of the time were often academies for smart youngsters. The hierarchy was rigid but there were good opportunities to rise within it. Over the next three years, J.P. sampled most jobs: rivet heater, steam tractor builder, service mechanic.

While J.P. was on a trip to the next province, his customer's neighbour looked in to ask what it would cost to draw up plans for an engine room, complete with power saw and mill. J.P. smelled extra money and, breathing not a word about his total lack of architectural knowledge, took careful measurements from which he produced a drawing.

Back in Eskilstuna, Director Munktell was impressed. 'Can you design too, son?' J.P. was sent down to the design office and given the job of drawing a tallow cup for greasing cylinders.

'I did it, too. Munktell's got the patent for them,' he seemed to let slip in an interview and then, jokingly to the reporter: 'And I also spent three months in prison.'

'???'

'Yes, installing a heating system at the Långholmen prison in Stockholm.'

At one stage, he almost embarked for America, but J.P. Johansson was not the adventurous sort. He hesitated, pondering over what he really wanted. Which turned out to be starting his own business. And

The first factory. Johansson had come across a little brook that could provide hydropower and in 1887 founded the Enköping Mechanical Workshop. Listed among the factory's services were: manufacture of forges and 'repairs for locomobiles'.

An advertisement for Johansson's clover-threshing machine – an invention that efficiently separated clover seed from its hull. The advertisement also announced the opening of Johansson's new factory by the little waterfall near Enköping.

In the bosom of the family. J.P. Johansson was a true family patriarch for children Inger, Gunnar, Märta and Brita (Tyra, Hannes, Judith and Ingrid) – and for his employees. He went to posterity as a considerate, well-intentioned father and boss.

Enköpings Mekaniska Verkstads

nykonstruerade, af framstående Landtbrukare och Teknici vitsordade och erkända såsom de bästa af hitintills i handeln förekommande

Klöfvernötningsmaskiner

för ång- eller dragkraft.

Säljas på fördelaktigaste vilkor uti

J. L. THORSLUNDS
Jern & Redskapsaffär.

where were his greatest opportunities for realising this – at home or in America?

In 1887, J.P. Johansson, now 33, bumped into his old employer, Munktell.

'How are you doing, Johan?'

'Fine, thanks. I have just bought a waterfall outside Enköping.'

'A waterfall? In Enköping? Where is it?'

'Just east of town, in the hills.'

'Of course, by that big garden! I lived with a family near there when I was young and used to steal apples from the garden. I remember the little brook down the slope. Congratulations!'

Others shook their heads. The factory was 20 minutes from the town, out in the countryside; what made him think customers would hike all that way?

'All the better,' said the new factory owner. 'I won't have to worry about old pans, pots with broken feet and jammed locks. There's no profit in that kind of work. Besides, I have always held that factories should be outside towns and away from dusty streets, for the workers' sake.'

While his wife Matilda was giving birth to four children in eight years – Tyra, Judith, Hannes and Ingrid – J.P. was founding an industry. The little repair shop out in the woods was about to become much bigger. There was frequent newspaper coverage about the inventive out-of-towner who had settled in Enköping and was always hiring.

5 October 1888: 'No fewer than 14 workers now appear to be employed at Mr Johansson's mechanical workshop at Fanna. New orders arrive ceaselessly, thus the staff will shortly be augmented even further.'

10 November 1896: 'The lamps ordered from Germany for the Enköping mechanical workshop under the ownership of Manufacturer Johansson were installed last Thursday, and that very evening spread light over the workshop premises. In more than one sense, the result was brilliant.'

And then, on 16 July 1897, only five days after his friend Salomon Andrée had taken off for the Pole from Spitsbergen:

'The entire staff of the Fanna mechanical workshop, about 50 men, will depart tomorrow by steamboat for the Stockholm Exhibition,

The Enköping Mechanical Workshop in 1899. Twenty-two years had passed since J.P. Johansson had started the factory with only six employees. The factory's popular, slightly squat boss is in the bowler hat in the middle of the front row.

'Old man Johansson' on Fanna Hill, 1902. The picture shows J.P. Johansson as he liked to be seen: a benign tribal chief taking care of his employees and their families. He was among the first to build company accommodation and schools. At Christmas, neighbourhood children were invited to his mansion to be given presents.

The advertisement that announced the opening of J.P. Johansson's new factory by the waterfall near Enköping.

Undertecknad,
som under 6 år tjenstgjort som maskinuppsättare vid Munktells mekaniska verkstad i Eskilstuna, verkställer uppsättningar och reparationer af ångmaskiner, tröskverk qvarn- och sågverk, mejerier m.m.; utför anläggning af rörbrunnar och vattenledningar samt reparerar alla förekommande landtbruksmaskiner. Godt arbete och moderata priser utlofvas.
Enköping den 3 juli 1886.   J. P. Johansson.

returning by boat next Tuesday. Director Johansson will pay for both travel and entry to the Exhibition for all concerned.'

One genius was flying a balloon while the other was travelling by steamboat. Andrée strove for the grandiloquent, J.P. Johansson worked on small, everyday things: in 1890 a 'clover-crusher' — two moulded trundles with nipples that 'could be pressed so tightly against each other that no seed-hull could leave the machine without being separated from its seed.' In 1891, it was a device for mechanical seed sowers. In 1894 a rotary press. In 1895 a spring hammer, which 'according to the needs of the smith, will beat or form in one minute both the thickest iron bar or the finest tin.' In 1897 'The Spring', a water trough that automatically regulated water supply and which won medals at several agricultural fairs.

He built an iron pedestrian bridge that delighted the town citizens it served. He became involved in local right-wing politics, with statistics indicating his advance up the nomination list for every mandate period.

On 17 January 1896, he announced through the local newspaper that 'as for many years on Twelfth Day, Director Johansson of Fanna and his wife have invited a number of poor children from the area for an afternoon's play and to "plunder the Christmas tree" and take home to their parents our heartfelt thanks.'

This was small-town life by numbers. The extensive interview given at Christmas in 1929 ended with a litany of tributes. J.P. Johansson was presented as an apple-cheeked, common-sense man of honour, with a finger in virtually every pie in his small home town. To be sure, he had sold his tool factory to his partner, B.A. Hjort, who would shortly tack on '& Co', twist the name a fraction and make 'Bahco' world-renowned. Still, the stocky, almost cubical 76-year-old chatting to the reporter among hall mirrors and piles of earthworms, was unequivocally the man of the moment in Enköping.

Safe and sound and ensconced in his wing chair, he smiled benignly at the photographer, remembering a life in which drama was always of the milder kind.

It would have been boring to the point of nausea were it not for three spectacular incidents.

10 October 1893: 'Manufacturer J.P. Johansson of Fanna was the victim of an attack on Saturday, when on his way home from town on his velocipede. Just outside the old customs boundary, Mr J. met

Johansson invented the Triplex Lamp in 1919 to help employees work effectively. Like all of Johansson's inventions, it was born from a practical, hands-on need. Let others dream of perpetual motion machines.

A business colleague, B.A. Hjorth, bought Johansson's tool factory and renamed the company Bahco.

TRIPLEX

Lill-
pendlar

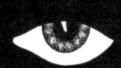

Smidiga
Eleganta
Oömma

arbetet skarpt belyst   *ögat väl skyddat !*

a man who grabbed him by his collar, with the obvious intent of stopping him. Using his velocipede as a shield, J. was able to liberate himself but in the attempt, fell into the ditch together with said vehicle. J. then heard his first attacker whistle to summon two friends who were quickly on the scene. Upon which, J. abandoned his velocipede and, shielded by the dusk, found his way to the horseradish field while the scoundrels searched high and low, swearing the while. Superficially muddied and lacking his cap, J. made his way back to town where the assault was naturally reported. The velocipede and cap were recovered and J. was able to regain his home unscathed. The identities of the precocious villains are unknown but Mr J. suspects a trio of badly dressed individuals he remembers observing him, preceding the incident, as he changed a fifty-kronor banknote in a shop.'

J.P. Johansson would have been able to depart this earth a lily-white man of honour had it not been for a black mark well hidden beneath his pin-stripe suit.

He may have joked about time spent in prison installing the heating, but the fact is, a far more serious reason might well have landed him in prison.

In 1908, Sweden was seething with labour unrest – to the extent that a ship carrying strike-breakers, the 'Amalthea', was blown up at dockside in Malmö, killing one and injuring 20 men. J.P. Johansson had been investing heavily in extensions to his workshops, had built his 'Fanna Castle' and bought a large coastal cruiser from another industrialist, B.A. Hjorth. Johansson was out on a limb financially. And there had recently been a burglary at his summer cottage at Ekolsund.

This was the backdrop when, on Sunday evening, 19 July, he returned to the cottage after a walk with his son. The garden boasted a large bower of Swedish whitebeam and maple; there, two friends and neighbours were waiting, the engineer Erik Kignell and District Judge Söderberg with wives.

Kignell, a father of two, was works manager at a local factory, Enköpings Maskinfabrik. He held 50 shares in the business, Johansson 13. The men knew each other well, their families enjoying each other's company frequently.

Under the headline 'A Shocking Incident with Fatal Outcome' the next day's edition of the local paper told how Kignell had had the unfortunate idea of playing a joke on Johansson. Kignell would

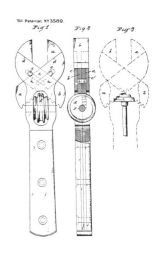

The adjustable spanner that was granted a patent on 24 November 1891. J.P. Johansson quickly realised that precision and durability could both be increased if only one of the tool's jaws was moveable. Six months later, he had created the wrench.

pretend to be one of those burglars Johansson railed on about. But unknown to Kignell, Johansson and his 20-year-old son Hannes had used their stroll to fetch a shotgun left on board the family's boat down at the lake. Possibly, the recent labour unrest had made Johansson upset and jumpy.

J.P. was definitely not a marksman. Plus, his eyesight was poor. When Kignell jumped out on him in the dark, J.P. reacted instinctively. A shot was fired and the local paper reported that it 'hit Engineer Kignell at a range of only a few paces and in the left side of the chest, proving immediately fatal …'

In 1886, Johansson lost his two-year-old boy Johannes Alexander to scarlet fever and diphtheria. In 1914, his wife Matilda died at 58, after ten years of bad health. These episodes framed the tragedy at the cottage. J.P. took the accidental shooting hard, but there was to be no judicial aftermath. All involved realised that the dim-sighted, agitated Johansson acted without malice aforethought.

The only apparent result was an intensification of his philanthropy. And when J.P. Johansson finally passed away on 25 August 1943, he was seen as the greatest son Enköping ever had – he was acclaimed, loved and admired. He had produced superb inventions – only in the years before he died: the pipe cleaner, the bicycle lock, fire tongs and the door buzzer – and had treated poor children to Christmas parties and presents. He had provided thousands with bread and work and, in the autumn of his life, had endowed the J.P. Johansson Scholarship to annually reward a 'well-behaved pupil with the gift of good comprehension, precedence going to pupils from less well-to-do homes.'

Forty-five years later, on 2 June 1998, his factory was to produce its hundred millionth monkey wrench. It was astonishingly similar to the first, 'Adam', forged in 1892 in a sunny, forest glade, where children tumbled from the kitchen steps into the green grass. J.P. Johansson's major invention was to a great extent fully developed the moment the first wrench left the anvil. This is both unusual and in a way grand. The only visible difference is that the angle has been turned 30 degrees between neck and jaw, the better to reach difficult places.

Today, the whole world uses his wrench. In Russia, it is even nicknamed sjvedik – the Little Swede.

A good name for a great invention.

MAN OF SPEED

Gustaf de Laval 1845–1913

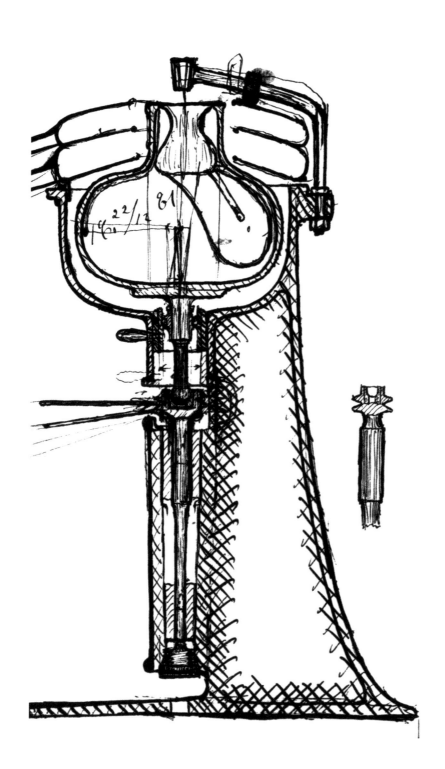

In 1913, when the estate of one of Sweden's most lionised industrialists was wound up following his death, his debts were reckoned at almost five million kronor (approx. $475,000).

The assets?

Nine hundred and seventy-three kronor (approx. $93), a diamond ring and a violin, both already pawned to an unhappy father-in-law.

The man of speed, Gustaf de Laval, had finally brought his runaway machine to a halt, too late.

Up until his death, he had owned 92 Swedish patents and 37 companies. He should have been a Croesus. Instead, the bailiffs had only recently emptied his wealthy home while de Laval vainly tried to jolly his young wife along: 'Heavens, we're not married to the curtains!'

But Isabel de Laval was in tears. It was as though a termite army had descended on them; their furnishings and trappings were disappearing out the door, borne by sweaty men from an alien class.

Such a scandal for a decent family!

But typical for Gustaf de Laval, who had lived his entire life as if there were no tomorrow.

That is, his tomorrow was a hundred years in the future. This was his strength and his weakness. Gustaf de Laval was the great visionary among Swedish inventors, a science-fiction figure who, throughout his life, despised routine and found the dreams of others petty and valueless.

His most famous invention was, nonetheless, something as mundane as a machine that separated cream from milk. But the sketches he pored over in his study were of flying machines and space rockets. And there was one dream he nursed all his life: to build a ship to cross the Atlantic in only ten hours. This monster – and it certainly resembled one – had a huge hull hidden under the waterline, housing a 'high-pressure air machine'. Air would be forced out through small holes in the skin of the hull, producing a layer of air to reduce friction. From the air, it would resemble a small, speedy motorboat humming across a large lake.

'A man of speed' is the legend on de Laval's gravestone in Stockholm's North Cemetery: speed created his empire and caused its fall. Speed seduced and shattered him.

It was an exciting, chaotic life.

The 'man of speed', Gustaf de Laval (1845–1913), created invention after invention that built on speed, friction and centrifugal force. His life was much the same. Luckily, his creditors were not as swift in chasing him. The man who became one of the richest people in Sweden died broke.

Previous page: Gustaf de Laval's separator which skimmed cream from milk, using centrifugal force.

This was not apparent when young Carl Gustaf Patrik de Laval was growing up in a remote army officer's residence in Dalarna province. The family was of French extraction. Grandfather Claude de Laval had a career within the war machine of 'the Warrior King', Gustav II Adolf and almost all the male progeny were military officers. Including Gustaf's father, Jacques, who however retrained as a surveyor and settled down to an apparently peaceful and industrious life on the edge of a forest near Orsa.

Gustaf's mother, Johanna, was from a family of civil servants and doctors. She was equipped with sound judgement and a thrifty nature – which unfortunately her eldest son did not inherit. She stretched the household budget by drafting maps and was proud to have some extra money of her own. On Sunday evenings, she would play the piano. Gustaf and his younger brother, Jacques, were given a proper education and their own stringed instruments.

Gustaf was born on 9 May 1845. He and Jacques shared a bedroom in the attic. Gustaf's favourite pastime seemed to have been building blade wheels for turbines and steam machines in his father's workshop. Gustaf was ambitious. Schoolmates remembered him as a grind who would not join in their snowball fights, preferring to stay indoors during breaks, studying. His mother said he was 'lively and a dreamer'. She worried that he didn't seem to be living in the real world, dwelling instead on strange fantasies.

On 11 May 1863, Gustaf graduated from school with top grades, despite frequent spells of unhappiness: 'If there is anything in this world that could destroy originality and independence of understanding and imagination, it would be this obnoxious cramming for exams!'

But of the 22 students who, three summers later, were to graduate from Stockholm's Royal Institute of Technology, Gustaf was the obvious leading light. His future seemed assured. But the business climate was poorer than for years and there were no jobs for engineers. With the help of a cousin's husband, he landed a sort of public welfare job: a monotonous drudge as a storekeeper for the Stora Kopparberg Bergslag mining company. His salary was 75 kronor (approx. $ 9) a month – sheepskin coat and thick gloves thrown in.

When spring came, Gustaf travelled to Örebro in south-central Sweden to try his luck working for Wilhelm Wenström, a building

The officer's residence at Blåsenborg in Dalarna province, where Gustaf de Laval was born on 9 May 1845. His father was from an old French line of military officers but had retrained as a surveyor in the province.

The de Laval family gathered for a portrait. The year was 1855 and ten-year-old Gustaf, furthest to the right, had already built his first miniature steam machine in father Jacques' smithy.

contractor (and father of Jonas Wenström, the inventor of three-phase electricity transferral), but was disappointed in having to spend time bent over a drawing-board copying other people's ideas. Gustaf felt sick and misunderstood. He also felt bad because his college grades in mathematics had been poor, even though he had excelled at everything else. That autumn, he enrolled at Uppsala University, with all a university town's opportunities and temptations.

It was like putting a fish into its right element. The next four years were a breeze, right up to the formal confirmation of his doctor's degree on 31 May 1872, when Gustaf de Laval, in his thick Dalarna accent, defended his 28-page thesis on 'Wolfram and Its Chlorine Compounds'.

And yet, the picture that develops in his meticulous diary is of a struggling soul. 'Would that I could become a noble person, the pride and joy of my parents, the glory and redemption of my country!' Young Gustaf de Laval was a very pious person, often calling on the Almighty for help. He was rigorously self-critical, plagued by guilt and often feeling sick with 'stabs of pain in the heart' and 'chest pains'. He attempted to banish his aches with exercise and cold baths. He had trouble finding true friends and was never invited to anyone's home. He was never in love and turned, to cool his burning lust, to girls for whom it was a money transaction.

He was not much use as a drinking pal, either: gloomy, introverted and nervy. 'Break that bad habit of socialising over liquor,' he wrote, and confided in his diary that he despised 'the raw, animal behaviour at these Uppsala parties'.

There were hints of a stark fear of dying before his work was done. What work, one might ask? Not his studies, certainly – they were a piece of cake. But subsequent life: everything he was to accomplish for the good of mankind. The densely written diary testifies to a conviction that he had somehow been chosen – not unusual for a religiously inclined youth.

When his sister, Elin, died on 4 April 1870, Gustaf de Laval subjected his own life to even deeper scrutiny. What if it were to be wasted? What if he were to die before realising his great objectives: coal mining in Skåne province, hydroelectric power on Göta River, a grandiose iron industry for northern Sweden, a coastal defence system with nitroglycerin charges speeding towards an enemy at 40 feet per second?

Young technology student Gustaf posing for the camera on Christmas Day, 1863. Now 18, he was astounding his teachers with his sharp intellect and quick-fire thought processes. But Gustaf himself was unsatisfied; he thought school sapped his originality. Besides, he was tormented by religious and moral anguish.

'Sweden must be foremost among nations in terms of both industry and general prosperity,' he wrote.

'With all certainty, northern Sweden and especially Lapland will be Sweden's California, lacking only its man and capital!'

Its 'man' was naturally de Laval himself. Others would have to put the 'capital' together. While Sweden's agrarian society plodded along at its ancient, treacly pace, Gustaf de Laval was pacing Uppsala's cobbled streets with his polished spectacles and downy beard, plans zapping like lightning-fast Atlantic steamers through his heated brain. Asphalt from the rocks at Hunneberg? Peat from the marshes of Småland province? A factory in Trollhättan to refine coconut oil?

In effect, he was sketching Sweden 100 years on. Wasn't his 'high-pressure air machine' rather like a jet engine?

All his life, Gustaf de Laval saw himself as a saviour of his nation, and his increasing eccentricity might be seen against this background. 'We must scale mountains of junk to advance!' he cried. He scattered aphorisms around him: 'From the seed of difficulties grows success!'

Or, in more real-life terms: 'What is a stupid promissory note against a machine that will take mankind to a higher plane?'

Prophets are hard people to live with. Gustaf de Laval made and broke promises, borrowed and then forgot. His business partners saw only his outer shell, a polished façade radiating calm and self-assurance. Promissory notes were signed only to lapse. Violins were pawned and IOUs stuffed into the back of desk drawers.

His great achievement was that he managed so well to keep up appearances.

When Gustaf de Laval turned 50 on 9 May 1895, a throng gathered outside his palatial Stockholm apartment at No. 27 Strandvägen to congratulate a nation's benefactor. De Laval stood statesman-like on his balcony, dressed in tails and with pomade glistening in his hair, every inch the empire-builder.

Only a few realised that the structural supports were rotten to the core. Not because of greed and avarice, but of negligence and a poor grasp of reality. 'All right, all right!' was Gustaf's usual response when Isabel ventured to mention the increasingly vulnerable family budget. 'It'll be taken care of. I just have to finish work on my new invention.'

'Are perhaps my plans and dreams of great deeds, power and

One of many rough draft sketches for the pioneering separator, which used centrifugal force to skim cream off milk. It was to be Gustaf de Laval's most renowned invention, even though he saw it as one of the dullest. Building jet-powered motorboats was more fun.

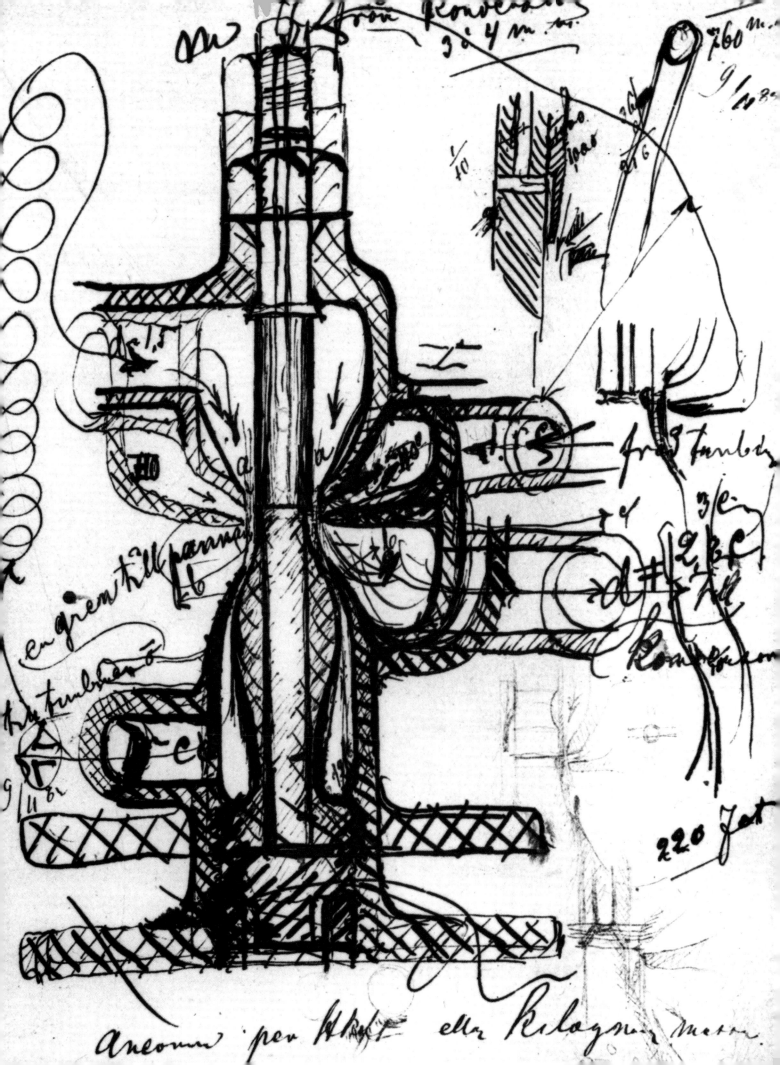

The ninth of May 1895. Gustaf de Laval's employees congratulate their benefactor on his 50th birthday underneath his apartment window on Stockholm's Strandvägen street. They see a thriving, prosperous industrialist who seems to be wading in money. But appearances were deceptive.

wealth only wild imaginings in a twisted mind, or am I really destined for greatness? Logic says no, yet I am inclined to disagree.'

When his breakthrough finally came, his reaction was vehement. All humility disappeared in a twinkling. Gustaf de Laval would be 'measured on a different scale than the world has thus far seen'. Self-pity was transformed into self-assertion. He had met the test; now he would show the pathetic small merchants of the world!

In 1876, he sent a friend to sell the Russians a warship that could sail at a fantastic 24 knots. The Russians were interested, until they realised that the boat had not been built. It was afloat only on the waves of de Laval's choppy mind. When they messaged de Laval that they would happily do business with him, but only when the boat had cast off from the dockyard of his imagination, he furiously told them to go to hell.

Nobody was going to put pressure on Gustaf de Laval.

Somebody who discovered this, although far too late, was a young Stockholm businessman called Oscar Lamm. Another young engineer, Alfred Hasselbom, who worked at the city's gasworks, often slept over on Lamm's office couch. One day, he announced that he had run into one of their old student chums at the gasworks.

'Remember Gustaf de Laval? He showed up today to demonstrate a separator that could extract ammonia from tar. I've asked him to come by. He says he has a heap of inventions. All he needs is backing.'

If Oscar Lamm had known more, he would never have let de Laval through the door. No one would invest in Gustaf de Laval's ideas because, despite his tender years, he was already carrying a debt of 40,000 kronor (nearly $4,000) after a spectacular bottling venture failure.

In 1874, he had been hired as an engineer at the Kloster glassworks in Dalarna province, charming all with his lively manner. He was a dapper young man who spent considerably on scarves, gloves, eau de cologne and fittings at an exclusive Stockholm tailor's. His accounts showed that he often visited 'the wiggery' where he would buy his pomade. One purchase was of a hat 'of genuine sealskin'; the entry indicated that the delivery boy had earned a tip. On one occasion he won 2.80 kronor playing cards, he paid 3.25 for bathhouse visits and 9 for curative waters. He was invited to skating parties,

Sketches of de Laval's 'air-cushioned boat' which, according to the inventor, would cross the Atlantic in ten hours. The craft had a trial run on Lake Mälaren near Stockholm and reached a modest eight knots. Many years later, it would be the subject of a legal tussle with an English hover-craft constructor.

The locksmith's work-shop at Kloster where de Laval threw all his ener-gy into an experiment to make glass bottles using a rotating mould. As with so many other projects, it ended in brilliant failure.

went to balls now and then but apparently bought only one book: 'Sweden's Industrial Establishment', a magnificent volume, handsomely illustrated.

The bottle factory was a typical de Laval brainwave, using extreme speeds and centrifugal force. The bottles would be made in swiftly rotating moulds. And it worked, but simultaneously, market prices dropped like a stone.

Only a single note in his diary, dated 11 p.m. on New Year's Eve 1874, referred to the failure: 'What a tremendous muddle this glassworks company was, and how naïve you were to get involved!'

At Lamm's Stockholm office three years later, de Laval delivered his full repertoire. In his briefcase he had the blueprints for another machine, also using the centrifugal force he was so enamoured of. From childhood, he recalled what trouble it was for farmers to separate cream from milk. During his final month at Kloster, he had pondered deeply on the problem. It had begun with an evening's entertainment at the glassworks, fuelled by cognac and cigars, with Director Lagergren producing a German magazine, 'Milchzeitung', and turning to an article about an engineer called Lefeldt, who claimed that the solution to the separation problem lay with speed and centrifugal force. The most beautiful of natural forces, agreed de Laval.

'Do you realise how much money one could make from a creamer like that?' exclaimed Lagergren, ever interested in technical progress. 'Or just in the milk industry itself? Now that towns are growing so fast.'

'Of course, but it could be made much better,' said the 32-year-old from his sofa.

So there he was at Lamm's office, with his invention complete. He had left the Kloster glassworks with the prophetic words: 'You shall be hearing from me!' But it had been a dire autumn. Not a single reply to his classified advertisement: 'Gentleman in his thirties with both technical and academic training seeks employment as manager or technical manager in a firm. Excellent testimonials and references on request.'

A single person was to take pity on de Laval – his cousin Tycko Robsahn, technical chief at the Liljeholmen Candle Factory. De Laval was given the run of the smithy, where there was a centrifuge for

A mobile milking apparatus that could be rolled out into the pasture was among de Laval's failed inventions.

An 1880 advertisement for a horse-driven separator.

The farmer's best friend. The hand-driven separator made an enormous impact on Swedish agriculture. Even today, old separators can be found in many country attics. The design was so simple and robust that many are still in perfect working order.

getting rid of fatty acids from candle grease. Power was from a 40-horsepower steam engine. On 16 December, he conducted his first successful experiment. Nine jugs of newly strained milk were poured into the centrifuge, rotating at 1,200 rpm. After fifteen minutes, 'the surface of the cream was as hard as butter'. When de Laval touched that surface with a stick, 'cream flew around like wood shavings'.

Oscar Lamm stared at the apparatus, fascinated. 'I'm in,' he mumbled. 'I'll go to the bank tomorrow.'

Lamm's father was less enthusiastic. He protested, but was ultimately unable to stop his son investing 4,000 kronor in de Laval's separator. Young Lamm closed the deal in February 1878 with the words: 'Gustaf my friend, from now on I'll look after the business while you get the machine working!'

Over the next eight years, 'friend Gustaf' would become a despised name. Although not initially. Sales were slow for the separator when it was first advertised on 15 January 1878, but in 1882, sales suddenly jumped to 560 machines and the two men were able to form a limited company, Separator, in 1883. Lamm was chairman of the board and de Laval the only other member. They had 100 shares each.

A year later, Gustaf de Laval launched his next big seller: a steam turbine with steam hitting a wheel and spinning it furiously. He claimed to have discovered the principle up at the Kloster glassworks, when an S-shaped nozzle came loose during sand-blasting and almost took a workman's head off. Gustaf de Laval was hardly the first to conceive this; in Greece in the first century AD, Hero of Alexandria described an aeolipile or steam turbine, but de Laval's 'rotating steam engine' was so fast and effective that the world was agape.

But all too soon, the firm was creaking at the seams. Gustaf de Laval was not the type to listen to others. He gave orders, did much what he wanted, and spent money. Even though he was getting 25 kronor (approx. $2.40) commission for every machine sold, he was in debt to the company to the tune of 6,000 kronor. His moodiness increased. He could burst into rages and abuse his partner. At times, he would disappear without word, only to be discovered days later, enjoying a cup of coffee at one of the city's finer cafés. Without seeking Oscar Lamm's approval, he started new companies for new inventions. His notebooks are full of drawings and comments such as 'Splendid! Apply for patent immediately!' and 'May perhaps work,

The body was often still, but the brain was always working at high pressure. Gustaf de Laval regarded his surroundings with slight disdain. Everything was too slow, too conservative. He, on the other hand, always had one foot in the future. De Laval left behind him 35 tightly written notebooks bubbling with ideas and prophetic thoughts.

even though it defies nature's laws.' To finance new devices, he would pawn Separator's assets and ultimately, his partner had had enough. The senior Lamm took over his son's shares, but found himself manoeuvred out in the spring of 1886 after what was in effect a coup by Gustaf de Laval.

Thus, one lamb went to slaughter and a new partner was hand-picked to take its place. Ekengren, a stockbroker, suited de Laval down to the ground; instead of nagging about money, Ekengren quickly penned a big, optimistic entry in the accounts for 'Expected Royalties'. But Ekengren did not last long either. Working with Gustaf de Laval was like living beside a volcano. At the drop of a hat, Director de Laval could boil over into violent fury, firing people left and right.

It is impossible to guess what sweet talk he used on Isabel Amalia Grundal, daughter of a doctor, but she presumably entered matrimony on the assumption that her husband was as prosperous as he looked.

He was 50 and she 21.

He had been a confirmed bachelor. Admittedly, he had been engaged to be married on one occasion, but managed to repel his beloved by talking of 'nothing but technology'.

The ageing genius and his beautiful young consort. The age difference is transparent in de Laval's notes; it was obvious that Isabel was the loyal ground staff while the head of the family was out changing the world.

'17 Sept. 1896, 2.30 p.m. Spoke to Isabel of flying machines.'

And a month later, in between a sketch and a technical formula:

'18 Oct. 1896, 7.45. It is a boy.'

Holding little Jacques Gustaf Adolf by the hand, he was later to be seen strolling along Strandvägen by the water's edge, studying the acrobatics of seagulls. The 51-year-old inventor had not given up his idea of a flying machine. But the unruly seagulls refused to fly the way Gustaf de Laval wanted. An irritated note in his diary: 'Seagulls obstinate!'

Even more obstinate were the creditors whose bills were piling up on his doorstep. De Laval would disdainfully sweep them aside with his foot. Not now! Maybe later ...

Paradoxically, this financial free-wheeler was planning to found a bank for promising young inventors. It transformed into an experimental workshop of some importance.

'My greenhouse,' he proudly called it. One of the protégés was the young Gustaf Dalén, working with his first inventions.

The inventors' nursery diverted attention from the spiralling loans, all the more like a manic separator. Sweden, with its reawakened ambitions of great economic power, needed this puff-chested, slap-dash genius. Everyone – at least everyone who had not lent him money – loved Gustaf de Laval! This was evidenced at the opening of the Stockholm Exhibition in Stockholm's Djurgården park in 1897, where the Separator stand was biggest, best and most attractive. Electric power was supplied by the De Laval Company's steam turbine, and light bulbs by the de Laval-owned Svea factory. The Sweden of King Oscar II wanted to take the new century by storm, and Gustaf de Laval was the perfect figurehead. He was showered in medals, inducted into the Science Academy and the Agricultural Academy and was lionised as a redeemer.

He also turned out to be a charming speaker, capable of 'capturing the audience's loyalty with his vibrant and humorous turn of phrase'. As an after-dinner speaker, he was less lucid. He often lost his thread and digressed into lengthy, technical speculation. Failing that, he might retreat to frankness in his thick, provincial accent: 'I won't know until tomorrow what I should have said today. Cheers, and thank you!'

A Danish newspaper described 'the Swedish miracle', with the writer ending his piece: 'But where will the monies come from? Everyone cannot be a shareholder in Dr de Laval's companies?'

Separator's shares were undeniably a marvel. In 1897, they increased almost twenty-fold in value. But while the foundations were being laid for a global company dealing in agricultural and alimentary technology, its front man was secretly battling huge debts.

The bubble burst that autumn. With repossession men literally knocking at the door of the Strandvägen apartment, there was no longer any way out. Everything of value disappeared out the door: couches, oil paintings, chandeliers and Persian carpets. To Isabel de Laval's nameless shame, the family was forced to move to more modest quarters. The man of speed had finally lost his footing and was slung out, centrifugally, into grief and economic ruin.

A happy family – perhaps only in appearance. In reality, there was a chasm between the hot-blooded Gustaf and the 29-year-younger Isabel. She had to suffer both his whims and public disgrace. Between them, their son Jacques.

Even though forced at times by insatiable creditors to leave the country, often travelling to London, he pressed on restlessly, coming up with invention after invention: helicopters, boats, peat machines, milking machines, rubber from dandelions …

Thirty-five notebooks have been recovered from the inventor's workshop, with urgent steel-nibbed pen racing across the pages, often at night when he sprang from his bed, tormented by yet another notion. In his old age, Gustaf de Laval was never without a current notebook, ready to be yanked from his attaché case to show the very latest to friends he met on trams or in cafés.

Under the heading 'Things to Think About for the Future' were hundreds of sketches and projects, from fireplace lighters to steam turbine-driven cars. Reading these would have made Jules Verne himself envious. When only 24, Gustaf de Laval had written prophetically, 'Power for air sailing will be direct application of combustive power from explosive matter! Successive combustion!! Analogous with rockets etc. and use of aerofoils.'

And a year later, 17 November 1870: 'What an important day in the history of human development! The inauguration of the Suez Canal! And achieved through the strength of a single man, Ferdinand Lesseps!! Progress has taken giant steps! How will it end? Shortly, man will fly with the speed of birds through space, and already human messages dash across the globe as fast as the mind can think!'

After an unsuccessful operation for cancer, he suddenly departed this life, a 64-year-old, destitute visionary.

A friend was quoted as saying, 'For de Laval, London was like the first stop after Stockholm on the train south, and New York was as close as Göteborg. Molecules and atoms were his ninepins and holes a fraction of a millimetre wide were like gaping cavities. He was among the first to push the theory that the world was our backyard.'

This was brought home in May 1961 when the British company, Westland Aircraft, launched the first hovercraft. The company came up against a problem when applying for the patent – a Swede had registered a similar idea in 1877. The vessel had even been taken for a trial run on Lake Mälaren, outside Stockholm, and had reached a speed of eight knots.

The man of speed had left behind a global company in the making,

A share certificate for the astronomical value of 10,000 kronor in the Gustaf de Laval Laktator Company. The inventor method of looking after his own finances was simply to avoid paying bills. He believed he had bigger fish to fry.

Gustaf de Laval's imposing factory on Kungsholmen island in Stockholm. In time, he would start 37 companies in Sweden and own 92 patents. Among the myriad projects that never came to fruition were an asphalt mine and a coconut oil refinery in southern Sweden.

hundreds of fantastic ideas – and thousands of outstanding promissory notes.

Plus an extraordinary, amusing, often unpleasant diary, still capable of stirring a reader with its sweeping ideas and its almost phobically twisted view of reality, where grand deeds mix with petty detail in a swirling, frothy brew.

Most revealing is perhaps a note made of one of many Sunday walks through Stockholm. The man who owed millions has just gone through another bankruptcy. His partners are furious. The bailiff is hot on his tail. Isabel is crying.

Upon which Gustaf de Laval sits down at his desk and, with careful pen, notes: 'Found a coin at the Locks.'

A 58-year-old man of the future, together with his beloved son, Jacques Gustaf Adolf. The bubble had burst six years earlier. The family had been evicted from their luxury apartment and bailiffs had taken away their chandeliers and oriental carpets. But de Laval had not given up. His latest plan was to build helicopters and extract rubber from dandelions …

MATCHSTICK MAN

Janne Lundström 1815–1888

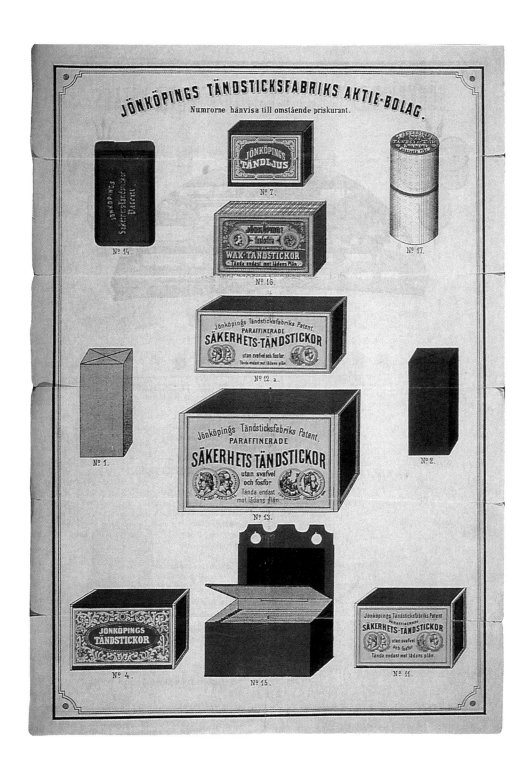

The stuff could rot your jaw off.

And there was the case of the housemaid, 24-year-old Sara Stina Johansdotter from Västernorrland province, arrested for the murder of her own child. She wanted to marry a man who was not the baby's father and the two-year-old was in the way. So she stirred a pack of match-heads into the baby's soup. The baby died in severe convulsions. The 1851 court record noted that the autopsy had found intact matches in the baby's stomach that, despite the elapsed time, 'could still be ignited'.

Throughout history, man has taken risks to provide himself with heat and light, but seldom were the risks as dramatic as at that time.

The reason was yellow phosphorous.

Phosphorous was the arsenic of the era. It was a super-dangerous chemical used to provoke abortions, kill weeds and rid the house of rats and mice. Prolonged contact would render the bones porous and brittle. There were cases of workers in the early match factories dying with rotting bones and collapsed joints.

This is the backdrop to the missionary accomplishment of the brothers Lundström. Janne Lundström was the visionary inventor, his brother Carl the hard-nosed entrepreneur.

One an ex-preacher, the other an exporter of such weird commodities as lingonberries, leeches and living capercaillie, or great wood grouse.

The capercaillie story is worth a digression simply because it is a snapshot of a time when nothing seemed impossible. Around 1840, Sweden was a Third World country and a poorhouse, but also the crucible of a new, revolutionary line of thought. Nothing seemed impossible. The world was yet a blank page and – who knew? – perhaps those hunt-mad Englishmen would pay good money for a stock of fowl to populate the woods of Sussex or Yorkshire?

Carl Lundström thought they would. He had read that the capercaillie was largely extinct in the British Isles. So he spent an entire summer visiting hunters in the forests of Småland province, famed for its rocky, forrested terrain.

And one fine day, there he was, on a boat headed across the North Sea, with a cargo chiefly made up of game.

A storm blew up. The capercaillie, accustomed to peaceful forest life, panicked. When the seas finally calmed, most of the birds were

The match baron who preferred the title of 'teacher' contributed to the transformation of Sweden from under-developed backwater into a leading industrial nation. Janne Lundström (1815–1888) was in fact an extremely conservative person who throughout life chose to use a quill. 'Long live the goose!' he would declare. 'She spreads our table, she makes our bed and with her young, we wipe our bums!'

Previous page: early products from the Jönköping Match Factory – the company that lit up an entire world.

dead in their cages. Despondent, Lundström dumped the cadavers overboard, and docked with the survivors. But happily, customers appeared wherever he turned! And they paid so handsomely that the expedition turned a small profit.

More importantly, the capercaillie adventure whetted Lundström's appetite for the export business.

It was an odd debut for the modern match. Its first showing outside Sweden was in the company of seasick fowl, sweet lingonberry mash in stone jars and leeches in glass. It's as though no one believed in the match. The good, tart berry and bleeding leeches were old-time Swedish specialties, but the match was a dark horse in the trading business.

Everyone knew that the match's small 'head' had caused many a tragic accident. Few were willing to believe Carl Lundström's claim that an invention by his elder brother would suddenly make matches safe.

To be sure, the substances involved could still take out half a small town, but the reason would be the human factor, not that the match contained deadly poison.

The safety match was born.

In 1851, dark, gloomy Sweden became the country that lit up an entire world.

Who were these first matchstick men?

To be honest, they were not the first. Man has been using fire for something like 500 million years. People had discovered that the coals left after lightning strikes or volcano eruptions not only provided warmth for cold caves, but could also scare off wild animals and singe meat to make it appetising.

About 10,000 years ago, people learned to produce fire using flint-stones or by rubbing sticks together, but it was not until the Greeks discovered the flammability of sulphur that the first item resembling the modern match was created.

Around 1670, a German alchemist and pharmacist named Henning Brand relieved himself in his mortar and observed that urine and sand reacted strangely together. What he was really after was the secret of making gold, alchemy. Instead, like so many others in that line, he stumbled on a completely different secret.

Brand had discovered yellow phosphorous, an extremely poisonous substance that combusts on contact with air. For the next 200 years,

yellow phosphorous would continue to entrance curious chemists.
One was the Swede Carl Wilhelm von Scheele, the discoverer of oxygen, who found a method to extract yellow phosphorous from crushed bone. Another genius was the Englishman Robert Boyle who tried mixing phosphorous with chemistry's old workhorse, sulphur, creating in 1680 the first match that ignited through friction.

Much progress followed.

The 'dipping stick' was invented; it ignited when dipped into a receptacle containing sulphuric acid.

An English pharmacist, John Walker, invented the 'friction stick', which admittedly was free from dangerous phosphorous, but, on the other hand, was extremely reluctant to catch fire even when rubbed on its rough sandpaper surface. One would often try stick after stick until some happy coincidence made one flare. It was hardly surprising that most households still depended on what was called a 'rope box': bound linen rags that would smoulder when the housemaid produced a flintstone spark. A phosphorous stick, applied to the smouldering rags, would ignite and be used to light firewood under the coffeepot on the stove.

Two Swedes would make contributions before the 'safe' match could finally ignite.

Jöns Jacob Berzelius is best known as the man who introduced modern chemical symbols and formulae, but he also discovered that yellow phosphorous could be replaced by red, which was virtually harmless. He would, however, never quite resolve its applications. The man who did was his countryman, Gustaf Erik Pasch, a gifted inventor who was later to perfect non-soluble cement for the trans-Sweden Göta Canal; produce a new kind of paper for currency notes; farm silkworms – and perform on the bassoon.

In 1844, Pasch patented a match that was neither poisonous nor liable to self-ignite in its box. Pasch had borrowed Walker's idea, replacing the sandpaper with red phosphorous. It promised to make him a fortune, especially when he became part owner of J.S. Bagge & Company in Stockholm, which since 1836 had been selling matches to eager buyers from a little hut.

Rarely have so many contributed so much to such a tiny invention. J.S. Bagge is also worth a mention. His original profession was as assistant teacher at Stockholm's College of Technology but he did not

3

Jönköpings Tändsticks-Fabrik

recognise boundaries between disciplines. The Board of Trade had granted him permission to manufacture products as diverse as razor strops, whetstones and eau de cologne. A newspaper advertisement, published on 7 October 1837, mentioned what were perhaps his most exciting products: 'Patented Chemical Sulphur Sticks, bound in lots of 100 pieces, wrapped solely in paper strips on which is printed Patent Sticks and a factory endorsement'. These, and 'Friction Lighting Sticks, unfailing, and of such quality that they retain their powers indefinitely'.

There was thus a lengthy overture before the entry of the Lundström brothers, but it gave a good indication of the often serpentine route to an invention.

There were eight years between the brothers. Johan Edvard 'Janne' Lundström was born in 1815, Carl Frans in 1823 and despite (or perhaps because of) different natures, they would remain fast friends all their lives. They were united partly by fear of their father, Johan Petter Lundström, a conservative book printer and newspaper publisher who seemed constantly to be fingering a cane. When the sons' mother died in 1863, Carl wrote to his brother: 'How empty it will now seem in our paternal household, now this great woman has deceased and a life of ideals, that only she could inspire, has fled our childhood hearth, leaving only his cold, dry, naked prose.'

Much later, in his old age, Carl would relent enough to thank his father for their strict upbringing, since that had saved him, Carl, from becoming 'a wayward ne'er-do-well'. Carl also wrote about the routine use of corporal punishment in schools, where every teacher kept a cane close to hand. Canes were used so often, wrote Carl, that they seldom lasted more than a week. To stutter while reciting one's homework was enough to justify a proper thrashing.

Janne had dreams of becoming an actor, but was packed off to Uppsala University to study for the priesthood. He was good at his studies, but had no vocation. His practice thesis was on mathematical graphs, not theology. He was drawn to the natural sciences but was also something of a whiz at classical languages. (Once later in life when hiring office staff, Janne called for applications written 'in a foreign language'. Perfectly reasonable for a company with business contacts abroad, although the successful applicant spoke neither English nor German, but Ancient Greek – a language that Janne himself had studied.)

The multi-talented inventor Gustaf Erik Pasch provided the base for Janne Lundström's creation, the 'safety match'. Pasch was fascinated by red phosphorous but also made the cement for Sweden's transnational Göta Canal, produced banknote paper and grew silkworms.

Sweden's first match factory. As early as 1836, J.S. Bagge & Co was making matches in its little Stockholm cottage – together with razor strops and eau de cologne.

A decorative label from the Jönköping Match Factory dating from around 1860. The Lundström brothers' company was one of the few to escape severe fire damage. Early on, the company installed sprinklers and hired night watchmen to check the premises.

This match-king-to-be was a real bookworm. He borrowed books from the Royal Academy of Sciences and corresponded with a learned book collector and librarian at Stockholm's Royal Library, Johan August Ahlstrand (who would later lend his name to Cape Ahlstrand on Spitsbergen Island in the Arctic Ocean). And by 1840, Janne was close to completing a dictionary of dialects from his southern Swedish province of Småland.

Carl was his elder brother's opposite. He never understood the point in learning such obscure subjects as Greek and philosophy. English was another thing altogether, since it could help him export goods and make money. But no private teacher of English could be found in all of Jönköping, their home and Småland's major town. Reluctantly, Carl turned to German and French, vowing not to waste his life at a dusty school desk.

While Janne exhibited bohemian traits, Carl was the single-minded strategist. He chose an education in trade and economics. When only 17, he was taken on as apprentice by a Herr Westerberg, wholesaler of Göteborg. Westerberg employed three clerks, all of whom slept in his home and ate at his table. It was practical, especially since the working day began at eight and ended no earlier than seven in the evening.

With the office closed and dinner finished, Carl would retire to his room. There he would devour his thick volumes, among them a book in German, 'Handbuch der Metallgiesserei' – a dry evening read for a teenager, but it prompted him to start thinking about starting a brass button factory.

The problem was that most such factories were in England. On the other hand, there were boats back and forth. So he hatched his mad plan to export grouse to finance a tour of inspection. And when the storm at sea had waned, and the surviving capercaillie had found new owners, Carl wound up in Birmingham. A manufacturer there was impressed with the enterprising northerner.

If the lad could sell poultry to the English, he could certainly flog buttons to Swedes. So it was a proud 20-year-old who returned to Jönköping, backed by a British manufacturer and with Jönköping's first steam engine in his luggage.

Janne was never to become a priest. He did actually preach one sermon, in the church of Hakarp parish, but was more interested

Carl Lundström, Janne's brother, shared the high forehead and the straight nose, but was a gung-ho businessman. He would sell anything: lingonberries, wild fowl, leeches, buttons and matches. He was not keen on matches that needed a striking surface; a 'well-travelled friend' had told him that this would not work in Africa, since 'the blacks won't accept matches that can't be lit on their backsides'.

His notebook indicates that Janne Lundström was a methodical man with ordered thoughts, but also some literary ambition. Lundström was always more a philosopher and generator of ideas than company boss. As soon as an invention bore fruit, he lost interest and hastened on to other things. He was never to become rich.

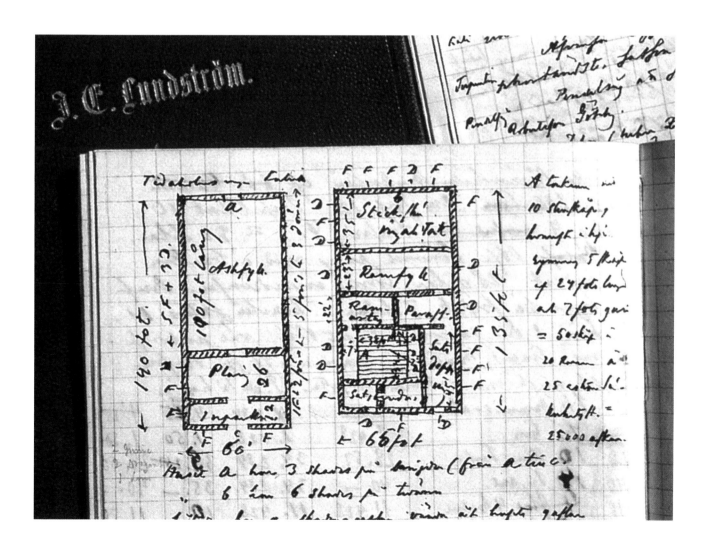

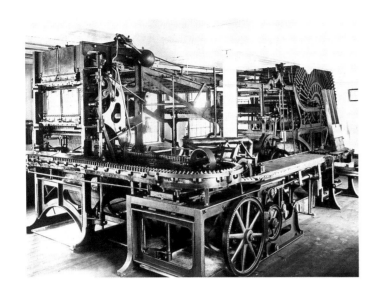

in the theological debate that raged in the local press.

As a young man, Janne had helped his father compose articles for his newspaper, 'Jönköpings Tidning'. Now the disaffected priest started his own, competing paper, together with a partner, chief bank clerk Johan Sandwall. 'Jönköpingsbladet' was a more liberal, free-thinking news-sheet and the editor eagerly embroiled himself and the paper in all current issues, not least the question of who should have representation in the Riksdag, or parliament.

Jumping to 1845, Janne Lundström decided that the brothers should set up in the match business.

It had been at the back of his mind since his student days at Uppsala. He might have known about Pasch's patented idea, but the foundation of what was to become an empire was that old (un)reliable yellow phosphorous. The trick was to make phosphorous sticks better and more cheaply. Sweden would ultimately have a total of 140 match factories, with at one time 40 operating concurrently.

The Lundströms' first move was to build a mechanical plane to supersede manual ones. So no one could copy their invention, the brothers ordered the parts separately from different factories, assembling the tool in their own. Industrial espionage was a popular occupation at the time. (Carl Lundström himself had visited a Malmö company called Malmros & Friis to see and copy their machinery.) Also popular was the shameless pirating of logos. Plagiarism was rife and the Lundströms were energetic in protecting their trademark and name: Jönköpings Tändsticksfabriks AB (The Jönköping Match Factory Company).

Next, they recruited carpenters by offering better pay. They also questioned whether pine really was the best material for matches. Wouldn't aspen wood be an improvement? It was easier to plane and did not splinter as easily. A working group of 'apostles' was immediately on the road, preaching aspen forestry to farmers and landowners. Every summer, Janne would travel north to Dalarna and Värmland provinces to check that enough logs were being floated down the great logging rivers.

A mill at Dylta supplied sulphur and a farmer, Johannes Svensson, supplied the Lundströms with glue for four decades, allowing him in time to retire in prosperity.

All this was on Janne's plate. The elder brother looked after the

As late as the turn of the 20th century, the manufacture of matches was still largely a handicraft. But machines were waiting in the wings. The Lundström brothers were far-sighted and courageous and their new machinery gave them a clear advantage over their competitors.

natural science part, while trader Carl went back to England to do a deal with Bryant & May in London through which they imported the brothers' matchboxes. These were few in number at the beginning, but the always inventive Carl packed all empty space on outgoing ships with lingonberries from Småland, and Newcastle coal on return trips.

They seemed set: business was solid and the customers loyal. But in 1852, a small red packet arrived on Janne Lundström's desk. It contained red phosphorous sticks, of the kind that Pasch had produced back in 1844. His patent had expired and besides, these were astoundingly better. The striking surface on Pasch's boxes had detached easily; on the new boxes, the striking surface was firmly in place after hundreds of hits.

The red phosphorous sticks were from Birmingham; a factory had found a way to produce the substance using an airtight oven heated to 200 degrees Celsius. Janne Lundström started thinking: could the striking surface be made even more effective and last even longer? He commissioned secret tests and soon held in his hand a swatch of striking surface that could be stored for years and still always produce an instant flame from a match.

The inventor was not completely satisfied. He could still be found sunk in his books or stirring chemicals over a burner. The factor that ultimately made his matchbox into a world-beater was an approaching world exhibition, to be held in Sweden in 1855. The organisers were desperate to find a Swedish invention that would astound the world. Somebody remembered a cache of matches in a storehouse, sealed and put there years previously to test their use-by quality. The boxes were brought out and tested and – Voilà! – every new match lit at first try!

It was a huge success, especially at the following Paris World Exhibition, where the Swedish safety match won a medal in the Hygiene Class and was touted as an environmentally friendly alternative to the risky phosphorous sticks. No more rotting jawbones, no murdered children, no more accidental bonfires!

At about that time, a Swedish diplomat confided in Carl that the brothers' matches would never be a big seller in Africa.

'Why on earth not?' asked a surprised Carl.

'Because I have heard that the naked Negroes of Africa believe that

Regulations for the Jönköping factory in 1854. Employees were urged to be disciplined and to be cautious with machinery and materials belonging to the owners.

Ordning ger framgång!

Då de flesta lådarbetarne på det oförswarligaste wårdslösa de spånor och öfriga lådämnen, som de hemta från Fabriken, och lådorna derigenom sedan en tid alltmer försämrats, måste, till förekommande af sådant, hädanefter owilforligen iakttagas:

1:o att alla lådämnen, spånor och etiketter icke få hemtas i knyten och påsar, utan böra de omsorgsfullt nedläggas i spånforgar eller lådor, i hwilka de kunna hembäras, utan att skadas.

2:o att hemtningen från Fabriken eller aflemnandet dit af arbete, icke får, såsom på sednare tider ofta warit fallet, ske genom små barn, hwilka icke utan största ansträngning kunnat bära de bördor, som pålagts dem.

3:o att wid lådtillwerkningen icke få anwändas andre personer, än sådane, som äro fullt skickliga och inöfwade dertill.

4:o att tillskuret papper eller spånor icke få, under arbetet, wårdslöst strös omkring, utan bör hwarje fort läggas ordentligt i sin hög. Spånorna äro isynnerhet de, som skadas af en wårdslös behandling: af dem böra på sin höjd 100 stycken på en gång framtagas till arbete: de öfriga måste ligga ordentligt qwar i sina högar, emedan de annars torka och icke kunna hoppassas till wackra stommar. Bäst förwaras lådorna, om en sten eller annan tyngd lägges ofwanpå hwarje hög och kring alla spånhögarne bredes en handduk eller ett kläde, som håller dem fuktiga.

5:o att icke flere omslag till spånor eller lådor på en gång få utläggas till klistring, än som kunna medhinnas att utan uppehåll göras färdiga. Ty om det utpenslade klistret får torka, förderfwas papperet, som då ej kan lossas utan att sönderslitas.

6:o att det blå papperet på den utåt wända sidan hålles så rent från klister som möjligt, annars uppkomma smutsfläckar, som göra lådan osnygg.

7:o att torkningen af lådorna sker i skuggan. Ty annars blifwa lådorna skefwa och bugtiga.

———

Den, som iakttager dessa föreskrifter, skall snart finna, att genom ordentlighet och renlighet en större färdighet i lådtillwerkningen winnes och att följaktligen en större arbetsförtjenst kan beredas.

Men de, som fortfara att wårdslösa arbetet, må skylla sig sjelfwa att de först få betala alla krokiga och smutsiga och rynkiga lådor, och sedan skiljas från ett arbete, som icke får wårdslöst skötas.

Jönköping den 1 Augusti 1854.

Tändsticksfabrikens egare.

matches will ignite if rubbed against the bare skin of a sensitive part of their anatomy!'

Despite such limitations, orders began to pour in from all corners of the world to the Lundström factory in Jönköping, on the banks of Lake Vättern.

This was a mixed blessing: how could they cope? The bottleneck in production was the drying process: the need to hang up each individual match to dry, at a secure distance from its neighbour.

By 1857, the Jönköping factory was still producing only 504 boxes a day. Ten years on, the number had, to be sure, risen to 15,000. But by the very next year, output was suddenly at 64,000.

The causes were a woman and a typo.

The woman was Carl's, wife Sophie. Reading the morning paper, she had found a strangely worded advertisement. When she called her husband's attention to it, he saw it was an ad targeted at match manufacturers, announcing a revolutionary machine developed by a certain Herr Gebold in Durlach, Germany. The description of the machine's function made no sense at all.

Then Carl figured it out: it had to be a typo. It must be a machine with built-in drying capacity – just what the Lundströms had been longing for.

Carl took the next train to Germany, returning swiftly with some of Gebold's machines and – most important of all – exclusive rights for Sweden. The foundation was thus laid for the factory's formidable expansion. Yearly production value increased 5,000 per cent between 1845 and 1860. Ten years later, it had increased another 500 per cent. By then, the number of employees had risen from 35 to 1,000.

It was not only the built-in drier that streamlined production; perhaps even more important was the 'complete machine' developed in 1877 by staff employee Alexander Lagerman to combine the work done by most of the other machines. It was a wonder and it scared the life out of the workforce. The Complete spat out 20,000 boxes a day – far more than could be produced by the 1,200 cottage workers who had fed the factory with boxes for years. There were special 'box bearers' whose only job was to make the rounds of cottage workers with deliveries of striking surface material, paper and glue, and return finished boxes to the factories.

The company employed a number of 'aspen apostles' – men sent out by Janne Lundström to convince forestry owners to fell aspen and transport it by river float to his factories. The wood was perfect for matches: it was not prone to splitting, it had straight fibres, had no resin sap and would not continue glowing after its flame was extinguished. According to legend, the aspen's leaves tremble because its wood was used for Christ's cross. Wits claimed the trembling was instead 'for fear of the Jönköping Match Factory'.

Many workmen were fearful of the Lundströms' mysterious new machines, while others were ready to adapt to modern times. The housewives who glued matchboxes at home ultimately lost their income. Meanwhile, the factory by the shore of Lake Vättern was expanding into an imposing complex in red brick.

Cottage industry always had a shameful taint. People who did gluing work kept quiet about it. But valuable income was threatened. Families around Jönköping quietly cursed Lagerman and the machine that could work 60 times faster than a pair of hands. In addition to the productivity increase, the Jönköping Match Factory was one of only a few not plagued by fires, thanks to built-in fire stations and fire guards patrolling the premises around the clock.

By the end of the 1880s, the Lundströms were bona fide match barons, and hats were respectfully doffed as the brothers strolled the streets of Jönköping.

Carl enjoyed the feel of his bulging wallet, but his elder brother would often have an absent look about him. Janne had always been the bohemian, the dreamer. He enjoyed inventing things – until they were complete. When the inventions were subsequently put to use, he would quickly lose interest. Making money was never an end in itself for him. His preserved bank savings book reveals that the director of one of Sweden's most successful companies had a balance that actually dropped by 98 kronor in the golden years of 1858–70. Bills and board meetings were boring irritations. He would have preferred the life of a poet, and he looked with envy on the flamboyant, romantic career of Carl Jonas Love Almqvist. Janne Lundström wrote cryptically in a letter that he wished he could 'walk in the footsteps of [August] Strindberg'. He may have meant it figuratively, or he may have been aware that, as a 14-year-old, Strindberg himself experimented with match production, before he accepted his higher calling.

Jönköping's pride. Between 1845 and 1860, the Lundström brothers increased their turnover by 5,000 per-cent. Carl enjoyed the money and the prosper-ous lifestyle it bought, with servants, bowler hat and cigars. Janne still dreamt of being a poet.

Jönköpings Tändsticksfabrik, Jönköping.

Janne Lundström was nicknamed 'the match priest'. He spent his days writing elaborate essays, filled with Latin expressions and quotations. In one letter, he asked a friend whether he intended to 'pursue bucolicus' at his cottage in the Stockholm archipelago. Not easy to unravel into: 'leading a lazy, country life'! On another occasion, he complained that handwriting was being made more mechanical by the use of steel-nibbed pens. 'No! Long live the goose! She spreads our table, she makes our bed and with her young, we wipe our bums!'

Arvid Sjöberg, manager of the Jönköping Match Factory, ironically poisoned by phosphorous in 1891.

This was all alien to Carl. He looked on aghast as his brother's restlessness drew him into new, unsafe projects. And just when the match factory was booming, Janne resigned. He founded the Munksjö Paper Mill company together with a legendary Swedish newspaper publisher, Lars Johan Hierta. And just as that project was coming to rich fruition, Janne sold his shares and moved on.

Janne Lundström would spend the last years of his life working on a new printers' copying paste he called Robur.

And when he finally succeeded, he sold his shares for a song …

Brother Carl would also later leave the match business, putting his energies into agriculture and politics. For Carl, money and the production of goods were life's central pillars, while for Janne they always seemed secondary. He never liked titles like managing director or general manager, preferring 'teacher', and not one found in classroom or pulpit, but rather one who taught Swedes to produce safety matches, straw-paper and copying paste.

Janne Lundström never married. He was fond of quoting Voltaire on the subject: 'Marriage is too serious a matter to be entered into after such a short period of consideration as a lifetime.' And yet there were indications that he was not immune to the opposite sex. Against himself, he used to tell the story of how, one morning in 1865, he saw a tobacconist he dubbed 'Miss Fiken' chase a young layabout from her shop, armed with an ice skate! He immediately jotted down a poem and sent it over:

At a certain cigar shop I know
Worked a fine and comely girl.
Bred gentlemen would bow
Or give hats a respectful twirl.

To every genteel client she tried
To sell her cured narcotic leaf,
Nor could her timid lip hide
A smile, sweet beyond belief.
But here comes a Bodisco, a crook
Gripping those rose-pink fingers, not in play.
But at him her ice skate she shook
And chased that ugly thug away.

(Bodisco was a Russian admiral who had occupied the Swedish island of Gotland in 1808.) Later that day, a few Havana cigars were delivered to Ludström, accompanied by a reply, also in verse:

I send you now some leaf narcotic
Its like you'll only find in climes exotic.
Take it as pay for your amusing rhyme.
But remember now, and for next time,
Please give crimson ink a rest,
Because red fingers I do detest.

The answer was, unfortunately, not the work of Miss Fiken; it was a practical joke, cooked up by two friends, Orvar Odd and the publisher Lars Johan Hierta, who happened to be in the tobacconist's when Lundström's poem arrived and recognised his handwriting …

Carl seemed always to feel a deep debt of gratitude to his brother for his genius, but there was also a trace of irritation at Janne's romantic ennui. Janne was often broke and it was almost always Carl who came to his rescue. Carl's elegy for his elder brother was both touching and revealing: 'On 17 July 1888, I lost my dear, unforgettable brother, who constantly showered me with so much brotherly love and with whom I shared, especially in my younger days and for many years, so much of fun and light. The stubborn work we shouldered together was done in such good understanding that it never led to any real conflict between us, though views may at times have differed over how best to execute plans. This happy relationship must partly have been because our characters so complemented each other, and that his impulsive, imaginative intelligence at times sparked my more sober and practical nature, and equally, my ways influenced his.

Proof that Swedish matches were soon popular abroad: a company price list from the early 1870s shows stocks of matches in warehouses in Paris, Paris, Bremen, Amsterdam and London.

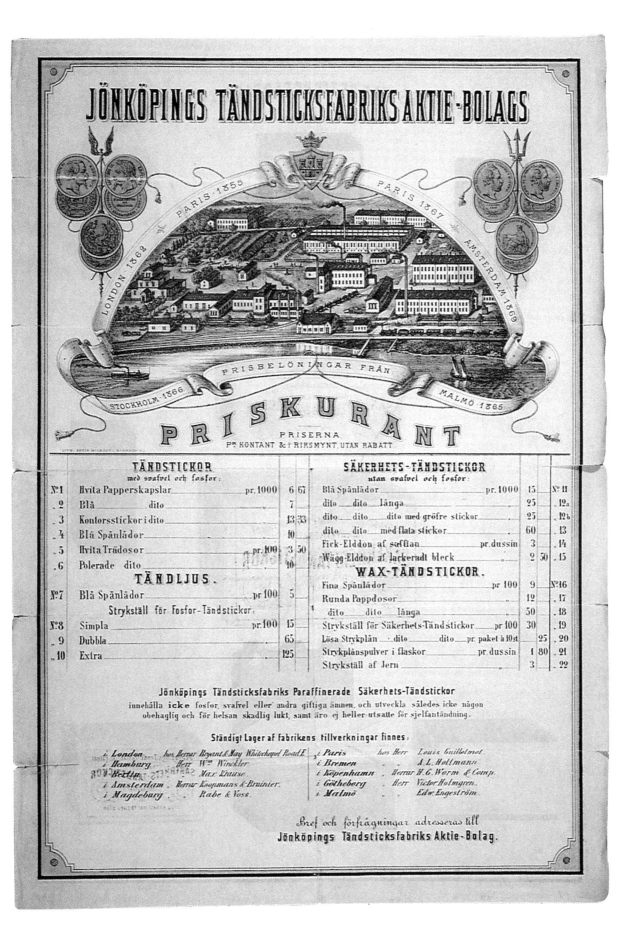

His loving sympathy also extended to my wife, our daughter and our family life.

In tranquil death, his unquiet spirit has finally found rest and peace. Without in any way finding fault, it was not possible to avoid seeing, and to an extent regretting, the unrest and changeability that accompanied his life. That unrest, I fear, made it hard for him to enjoy the fruits of the work to which he gave such attention and intelligence. His changeability partly stemmed from a lack in him of several qualities indispensable to the businessman. When in his ventures he found himself alone in deciding economic issues regarding production and sales, he did not achieve satisfactory results.

In private life, he was simple and moderate, loving what was thorough and without luxury; he was faithful to friendships and quietly joyous, when darker thoughts were not burdening him. He had no liking for the quarrelsome battles of municipal political life, where – unlike me – he declined all public duties. But foremost: he was a good man, with warmth within him for those in suffering and whom he often, discreetly, tried to help as much as he could.'

Janne Lundström once described himself in a letter to his brother in 1885: 'And how many are they, who follow life's path rationally? I could be an example of those who did not. As I now enter my 70th year on earth – which happens also to be the Match Factory's own 40th anniversary, this 28th of April – it could be said of me that "he tired halfway".'

What never tired were his famous matches.

Between 1845 and 1901, their formula was totally intact. Then came the impregnated match-head, which solved the problem of spitting sparks and smouldering embers. By then, the Lundström brothers had long since jumped ship – now a considerably less stable ship, steadily losing customers because of rigid price policies. A solution came with the merger with the company's toughest competition, the Vulcan Company. In 1917, the new company was itself swallowed up in the burgeoning Kreuger empire.

What became of the housemaid who murdered her baby?

After a lengthy period behind bars, she was ultimately pardoned and lived out her days as a farm housekeeper.

Burnt out and discarded like a used match.

The safety match spread across the world like a prairie fire. The picture shows a small sample of all the exotic labels that helped market Swedish Match Company products.

DYNAMITE MAN

Alfred Nobel 1833–1896

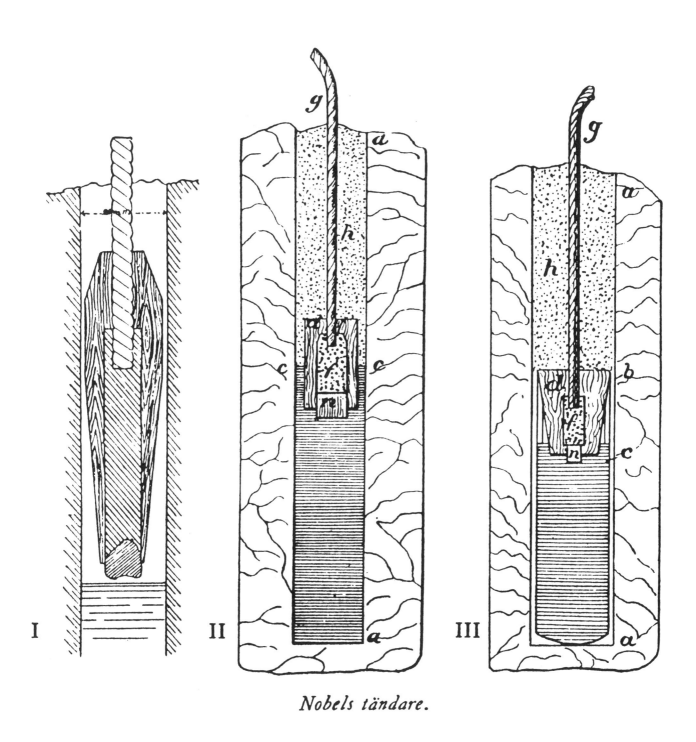

I   II   III

Nobels tändare.

In 1887, Ludvig Nobel asked his 54-year-old younger brother Alfred for a short monograph of his life, and received the following by mail: 'Alfred Nobel: pathetic semi-person, should have been suffocated by any humanistic doctor at the first, squealing evidence of life. Greatest qualities: keeping his fingernails clean and never depending on anyone. Greatest faults: lack of family, equable humour and calm digestion. Greatest and only desire: to avoid being buried alive. Greatest sin: not worshipping Mammon. Important events in his life: None.'

And as a coda: 'No one reads essays on people unless about actors and murderers, especially the latter, whether their achievement was on the battlefield or indoors in a manner to make people drop their jaws.'

It is an extraordinary document.

In human terms, Alfred Nobel should have been at the acme of his life. He was one of the world's richest men, guest of presidents, inducted into academies, a personal friend of Victor Hugo's, the lover of an 18-years-younger woman, and with his inventions shaking the world.

Nonetheless, his pen was brimming with bitterness that evening. In the darkest of moods, he sat at his writing desk at Avenue Malakoff 53 in Paris, reflecting on a lifetime that filled him only with disgust. Everything had been meaningless. Everything he had striven for had been a lie, a circus act, a despicable farce. Life had no meaning, no goal, and if there were a God, He was toying with his creation in a slapdash, malicious way.

'It would be almost pitiful to want to become someone or something among this motley collection of 1,400 million two-legged, tailless apes, loping around on our spinning projectile.'

Alfred Nobel never touched alcohol but drank deeply of the wine of self-hatred. Nobel never smoked, but over his prosperous villa hung a black cloud of despair. Nobody ever heard him laugh. There is scarcely one photograph of him even smiling. Mostly, his expression is melancholy, his eyebrows a sorrowful V. And yet, he was a man of contradictions.

In the Paris dawn, the voluminously bearded Swede could be seen striding along the boulevards, wrapped in warm fur and beset by an energy that glinted through his clear blue eyes. The dejection of the previous night had been swept away and he was again on his way to his laboratory and new experiments, new discoveries. Creativity was

World-famous but shy, a maker of cannon but a pacifist, as ingenious at the drawing board as he was pathetic at love and love-making. Alfred Nobel (1833–1896) was a man of huge contrasts. The man who wished so much good for the world also gave it blood, death and maimed limbs.

Previous page: Alfred Nobel's sketches for his detonator – perhaps the greatest of all his 355 patented inventions. The detonator was activated by a lit fuse to release the enormous force of the nitroglycerin. Only with this invention were all the world's great tunnel and railway constructions made possible.

his best psychotherapist. Constantly curious, constantly thirsting for
fresh knowledge, he flung himself out into the crowd and carved
a furious path through the awakening capital.

He was snowdrift-pale, this son of the North. Sickly and presumably hypochondriac, he would dash between spas and specialists all
his life, looking for relief from aching muscles, sudden fainting spells,
nosebleeds, rheumatism, migraine, insomnia, cold sores, poor digestion and 'piercing pains in the heart'. He would disappear for days or
weeks, returning in dark glasses and with his head swathed in band-
ages. When his brother, Ludvig, died in April 1888, Alfred suffered
a cramp attack, temporarily paralysing him.

This is perhaps the background to his fear of being buried alive.

Which was far from unique at the time. Medical science debated
the point of exact separation between life and death. The press drooled
over stories of excavated coffins with fingernail scratches on the
inside. Some of Edgar Allan Poe's best short stories were about people
buried alive and there were even designated reawakening clinics, where
bodies were kept for several days in order to avoid macabre mistakes.
And didn't Alfred Nobel's own father, Immanuel, invent, as early as
the 1840s, an alarm system for coffins for those still not dead to signal for help should they awake, six feet below?

Alfred was not about to take any risks. Meticulous in his approach
to everything in life, he left exact instructions in his will: 'Finally,
I decree as my express wish and command that after my death, my
arteries be opened and when this is done and visible signs of death
are established by competent medical staff, my body be incinerated in
a so-called cremation oven.'

Burned and destroyed. Yet another tailless ape ending its pathetic
earthly sojourn.

Regarding his decorations, the will was crass and bantering: 'I have
my cook to thank for my Swedish North Star Order, as her skill
appealed to high-born stomachs. My French medal came to me
because of my close acquaintanceship with a government minister.
I should gladly be spared such baubles and tin devices.'

Against this background, it is paradoxical that every year a magnificent party is thrown in Alfred Nobel's honour, an extravagant ball
where geniuses and royalty trade flattery and gorge themselves in
his memory.

'Europe's richest tramp'
on a visit to the aque-
duct at Dolce Acqua
Arma di Taggia in Italy.
Alfred Nobel would
later settle in that country after being falsely
accused of espionage by
the French authorities.

But Nobel was in every sense a mystery, a paradox, a contradictory, evasive person, mocking researchers these hundred years:

- continually sick, but with unstoppable energy
- generous to his friends, but brusque and silent in gatherings
- poorly schooled, but with a clear intellect and an impressive library
- a classical capitalist and opponent of female suffrage, but otherwise an anarchist and almost liberal in his zeal for reforms
- a realist, a pessimist and a scientist, but also a high-flown poet and writer of bombastic, pretentious literature

And perhaps most important of all:

- an inventor of deadly forces, but at heart a dedicated lover of peace

One incident affected Alfred Nobel like a brutal awakening. Throughout life, he had harboured the belief that humanity cherished him as an apostle of peace. That was to be one of the ramifications of dynamite: weapons would be so terrible that no government would dare use them, and 'war would thus forever be made impossible'.

But in April 1888, a Parisian newspaper published by mistake the obituary of 'le grand inventeur suédois Alfred Nobel'. It was in fact his elder brother, Ludvig, who had died. Too late, the newspaper realised its error, making Alfred Nobel one of the few who have read their own death notice.

It was devastating reading for Alfred. Not because he was thought dead; he had long lived with the idea of death. But the article called him 'The Merchant of Death', a man who made his fortune through the suffering of others. His inventions were, to be sure, used to open the St Gotthard Tunnel, linking people, and his dynamite had equally certainly contributed to increased prosperity, opening up seams of hidden ore, creating factories and jobs.

But he was remembered for his weapons. He had done the basic development work for grenades and warheads. What were conceived as tools of peace had 'sunk to contemptible instruments of murder'.

Suddenly, he saw all his blotches, wrinkles, weaknesses and failings as under a painful searchlight. All his life, he had shown rock-hard self-discipline to hide his tightly strung nerves. He moved easily between five languages, gave lavish dinner parties, was able to work for weeks at a stretch — but inside was a tangle of emotions, pushing and pulling at him.

He would visit his factories only on Sundays. Few of his employees had ever seen their chief. 'To act, not be seen,' was his dictum. When one of his personnel managers requested Nobel's portrait for an anniversary brochure, the answer was blunt: 'The day my colleagues, every last working man, can send their own portraits, I will add some reproduction of my own bristly bachelor's countenance to that collection, not before.'

Democrat, idealist, pioneer, seeker, businessman, lone wolf, cosmopolitan.

But who was the real Alfred Nobel?

The answer comes only in the form of an incomplete jigsaw puzzle. Some pieces fit, others seem to have been included by mistake. A clear part is the picture of Nobel's father, who put an early stamp on the family through indefatigable energy, brave plans — and repeated failure.

Immanuel Nobel was a tight knot of energy. Born in the coastal city of Gävle, he found himself as a 14-year-old on a sailing ship bound for the Near East, already learning that the world was an opportunity, not a threat. When 17, he became a builder and began to experiment with transportable wooden houses, pontoon bridges and new machinery.

Inventing amused him. In 1828, he took out a patent on 'Nobel's Mechanical Movement', which turned out to be a laundry mangle. In 1835, he founded Sweden's first rubber factory, marketing among other items an inflatable mattress, a then unheard-of creation.

The Nobel family tree had fascinating roots. One ancestor was a remarkable professor at the University of Uppsala, Olof Rudbeck. He was the most multi-faceted scientist of Sweden's 'Great Power' era (1611–1718) and the discoverer of the lymphatic vessel. He also attempted to prove that Sweden was the mythical Atlantis, the cradle of civilisation. Immanuel Nobel had undeniably inherited something of his ancestor's ostentatious, uneconomical, larger-than-life personality, while wife Andriette was his opposite: a down-to-earth, pleasant and practical woman, whose penchant for quick action also saved the family from a fire in 1832.

The family was not well off. Immanuel Nobel's business ventures

Nobel's mother, born Andriette Ahlsell, ran a vegetable grocery in Stockholm and fought to maintain standards, despite her husband's unlucky business ventures. She was said to be wise, good-hearted and cheerful.

Alfred's father, Immanuel Nobel, was an astute and optimistic autodidact whose inventions included a laundry mangle and what may have been the first inflatable mattress.

were disastrous. The family was forced to move frequently, to ever-poorer accommodation. The boys were sent out to sell lucifer matches on the street corners near Stockholm's central Norrmalmstorg square. Only four of the eight children would live to adulthood. But the marriage would survive for 45 years with no major crises.

When her husband abruptly announced one day that his company had gone bankrupt and that he would have to move to Finland alone, she simply packed his bag and gathered the children for an unsentimental send-off.

Their third son, Alfred Bernhard, was their worry. He was born on 21 October 1833 and was an unusually spindly little rascal. When he started school, he was sick from the first day and completed only two terms. (Later, in Russia, he would be more successful.) Little Alfred was, however, both sweet and smart. In his 1842 report card, he was among only three pupils (of a total of 82) given highest marks in application and behaviour.

Luck finally turned for Immanuel Nobel. His letters home revealed that he was now enjoying success as an architect and builder in Turku, Finland. In the early 1840s he moved to St Petersburg where he caught the eye of the Tsar. Nicholas I was a classic autocrat, quick to violence and decree. But the Swede interested him. Because what did this talented foreigner have in his back pocket if not an appealing military weapon!

While in Sweden, Immanuel Nobel had already invented a new kind of mine, but had been treated snootily by the military when he offered to show them the plans. Now, the Russians had requested a demonstration and the cascades of water in the Neva River implied the beginning of a new, happier period for the Nobel family.

By 1842, father was in possession of enough roubles to be able to send for his family. In October, nine-year-old Alfred arrived in his new homeland via sailing ship and coach. He was immediately placed in a Russian school, where he learned the language in no time at all. Russia acted as a stimulus for his intellect, imagination and zest for life. Sent abroad in 1850 as a 17-year-old on his first study tour, Alfred carried great expectations on his thin shoulders. The tour lasted two years and took him to see among others the great chemist, Pelouze, in Paris and the Swedish inventor, John Ericsson, in North America. Letters home indicated an extreme talent for observation but

Alfred Nobel's austere birthplace, No. 11 Norrlandsgatan in Stockholm. Alfred's mother sent her sons around the neighbourhood selling lucifer matches.

Next page: The Nobel family's finances were secured when Tsar Nikolai I expressed approval of Immanuel Nobel's underwater mines. Young Alfred was sent by sailing ship and coach to attend the blasting trials on the River Neva at St Petersburg. This watercolour is by Immanuel Nobel.

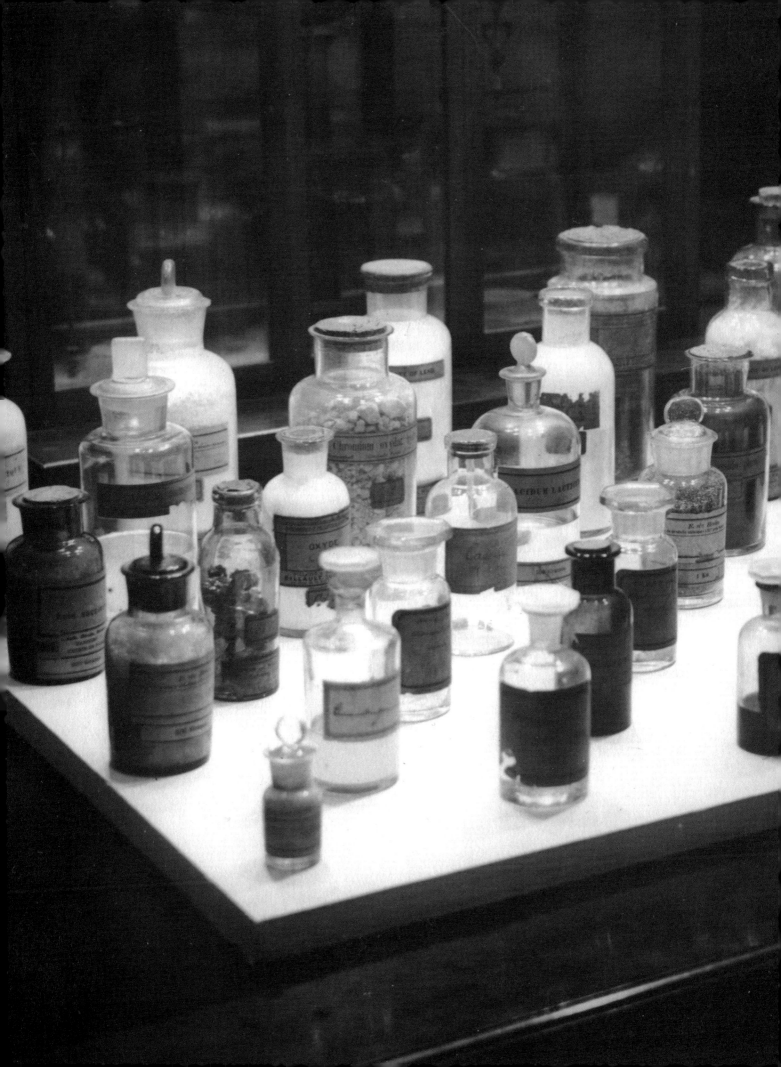

Chemicals in Nobel's laboratory in Sevran, outside Paris. He would hasten there on horseback at dawn each day, eager to tackle his latest daring experiment. Here, Nobel invented ballistite, the smokeless powder that gave riflemen better battlefield vision and permitted revolver duels.

Alfred Nobel's new weapons factory in Karlskoga was the hub of a revitalized Swedish defence industry. But by now, the ageing Nobel found Swedish winters too harsh, and was not present to witness the test firing of the factory's first 25mm cannon, vociferously welcomed by the hawkish monarch of the time, Oscar II.

Brothers Alfred, to the left, and Ludvig Nobel as fashionable young gentlemen in St Petersburg. Since foreigners were denied access to public education, the brothers studied with private tutors who were overjoyed at their aptitude.

also the precocious, dreamy introvert who favoured solitude. In 1858, he was sent off on a new trip – this time to dig up creditors for his father's company, again on the skids.

The Crimean War, 1853–56, had been a godsend for Nobel & Sons. Now, in peacetime, there was no demand for mines. Alfred returned empty-handed, forcing Immanuel Nobel back to Stockholm, while 26-year-old Robert, 24-year-old Ludvig and 22-year-old Alfred remained in St Petersburg. Ludvig had saved some money and wanted to open his own workshop.

It was there, in a simple little Russian kitchen, that his younger brother conducted the experiment that was to change the world.

Alfred had got the idea from Professor Pelouze in Paris. The professor had shown him a new material called pyroglycerin, prepared from nitric acid, sulphuric acid and glycerine. It was highly explosive, auto-combustible at 180 degrees Celsius, sensitive to sudden impacts, but could not be made to explode with a fuse.

Immanuel Nobel had listened attentively to his son's account. While Alfred mixed concoctions in his samovars, his father was doing his own experimenting in Stockholm. He called the resulting material 'nitroglycerin' and invited the military to view it. They, however, were just as off-hand as for the earlier experimental mines. This nitroglycerin was far too unstable, they stated. It could explode mightily, but at times not at all.

The breakthrough came on a spring day in 1862. The three Nobel brothers were standing by the canal outside their workshop, with Alfred holding a tin pipe in his hand. He lit a fuse, lowered the pipe into the water, letting the current carry it away. After a brief while, the pipe sank.

'Should we take cover?' asked Robert and Ludvig.

'No. No need,' replied Alfred, counting silently to himself.

When he came to 28, a dull thud was heard, and the water in the canal rose. After more than 50 failed attempts, Alfred had figured out that the nitroglycerin's weak point was the firing powder. He had then made a little copper capsule with detonating mercury, exploded by fuse. He called it a 'percussion cap' and it was to be perhaps the most important of all his 355 inventions.

The Nobel family business took off anew. Mining companies, tunnel builders, the military – all wanted the new blasting oil. While

The first page of an 1864 instruction booklet on the use of nitroglycerin. Not a word of possible risks.

Reglor för användande af Nitroglycerin
(patenterad Sprängolja.)
———

Nödiga redskap.

1:o Såkallade *tändare*. De bestå af en ihålig träd-cylinder, i hvars öfre ända stubinen instickes, hvar-efter hålet fylles med gevärskrut och täppes med en kork.

Sådana tändare jemte tillhörande korkar, finnas af nödiga dimensioner från 0,5 till 2,0 tums diameter.

Färdigladdade tändare, hvari blott stubinen be-höfver instickas, kunna äfven erhållas.

2:o En *jerntråd* för att mäta huru djupt sprängoljan fyller i borrhålet.

3:o Ett *graderadt mått* rymmande 1 ℔ sprängolja, hvarpå hvarje 10 ort kunna afläsas.

4:o Ett *långt rör* hvarigenom oljan hälles i berghålet för att ej förspilla någon del deraf som kunde qvar-häfta vid hålets öfre väggar.

5:o *Patroner* för horizontala eller ligg-hål.

Robert and Ludvig made their fortune as oil tycoons in Baku, Alfred chose to reunite with mother and father in Stockholm, where the family bought a town mansion near Långholmen Island.

'Nitroglycerin? Isn't that awfully dangerous?' people asked.

'Not at all,' proclaimed Alfred Nobel, demonstrating by touching a lighted match to the blasting oil, which burned with a slow, clear flame.

From a height, he would then throw a jar of the substance to the ground to show that the renowned contents could tolerate the hardest of knocks. The company's sole problem was in producing enough nitroglycerin to meet demand.

Then came the tragedy.

In the summer of 1864, Alfred's younger brother, 22-year-old Emil, was mixing nitroglycerin when a violent explosion tore the factory apart. Only a gaping hole remained of the laboratory where Emil and a friend had been working. Immanuel Nobel took his son's death hard. His large frame shrank and he retreated to his bed. Alfred, too, struggled with great feelings of guilt, but ultimately was able to pull himself together.

At the time, few inventions were so surrounded by myth as the yellow, glutinous nitroglycerin. The United States planned to ban it, which would have meant a huge financial loss for Alfred Nobel, who in the autumn of 1864 formed the Nitroglycerin Aktiebolaget company together with a wealthy partner, J.W. Smitt.

Alfred Nobel planned a sales tour to the United States, but just before he was to leave, a crate of nitroglycerin exploded in a New York hotel. A German visitor had left the crate in reception, where it was used as a seat and a footrest for shoe shining. 'The New York Times' had covered the American Civil War and the murder of Lincoln with single-column articles but now unveiled its first two-column headline.

To get his dangerous goods into the US, Nobel was now forced to smuggle it in hatboxes. Shortly afterwards, there were several new explosions: a large cargo of nitroglycerin on a German ship, in a Sydney storage, in a San Francisco warehouse and on a British cargo vessel.

Alfred Nobel would now play all the cards in the rich deck of his talent.

The shipping note for a delivery of nitroglycerin from the Hamburg factory in 1865.

As an inventor, he was clear-sighted, realistic and daring. Now, it was the student of human nature, the tactician, the man of eloquence at work. He had a magnificent courtroom presence, constructing his defence with elegance. He confirmed the spirit of the times: Higher! Further! Faster! Bigger!

'You cannot expect that an explosive substance can be put to public use without the loss of life. A simple review of statistics would show that the use of toy rifles causes proportionately more accidents than this substance, which is also a great and valuable aid in the exploitation of our mineral resources.'

Nobel was fighting on two fronts: the authorities must be appeased and he had to quickly find something to stabilise his nitroglycerin.

In his letters, Alfred Nobel was a brilliant stylist: earthy, sarcastic, funny, quick and sharply accurate. The Swedish Riksdag or parliament was 'a house of braggarts', journalists were 'two-legged germs', lawyers 'bloodsuckers', doctors 'academic jackasses'. His own aches and pains were 'best wishes from the Devil' and spas 'anatomy museums for worm-ridden corpses'.

When somebody asked permission to name a steamship after him, he declined, saying it must be 'a bad omen to christen her after an old wreck'.

In a dispute over a patent, he noted sardonically that, as usual, the establishment was following mankind's eleventh commandment: 'Thou shalt not improve!'

Alfred Nobel was guided by another set of principles. In the autumn of 1866, he was at a factory in Hamburg, in a purposeful search for something that could stabilise nitroglycerin without reducing its explosive force. Coal, cement, wood-flour, sawdust – nothing worked. Instead, the River Elbe and a flesh wound put him on the right path.

The river flowed past the factory, its banks covered with a kind of sand that absorbed moisture. It was kieselguhr, his chemists told him, a kind of silica composed of fossilised algae. 'Silica could be the answer,' Nobel said, and mixed it with his blasting oil until he had a dough that he could shape with his hands.

Nitroglycerin had found its stabiliser. Dynamite was born.

But despite the world renown that the new invention gave to Alfred Nobel's companies, he was still unsatisfied. Explosive force was less than he had hoped. And besides, the dynamite would not work in

A cargo of dynamite. A scene at the Vinterviken 'factory of death' in the early 1880s. But Alfred Nobel was able to calm nervous critics; one of his favourite tricks was to set fire to a jar of nitroglycerin while holding it in his hand.

The vanity case Alfred Nobel used to smuggle dangerous substances across borders. Panic ensued when a case filled with explosives blew up in a New York hotel lobby. It was not the inventor's case.

water. A solution came by chance. One day, he cut his finger, and an assistant covered the wound with a thin layer of ointment, the equivalent of a thin, transparent plaster.

That night, the ointment rubbed off. Sleepily, Nobel got up to find the jar. Curiosity made him study the label and then look up the active ingredient, collodium, in a reference book. 'Also known as gun cotton' the entry read. Gun cotton! What if he were to replace the silica, which had no explosive properties of its own, with gun cotton?

The new substance was given the name gelignite and was not only as effective as nitroglycerin, but it also worked under water.

Now, nothing stood in the way of Nobel's empire-building. But money was not his prime mover. With equal intensity, although perhaps less success, he worked on other sides of his personality.

Alfred Nobel's hero was not a scientist but the English poet, Percy Bysshe Shelley. Nobel not only committed long passages to memory but also tried to write verse of his own in the same spirit. Then it was the turn of Voltaire, whom Nobel translated into Swedish, before trying his hand at his own novels, 'In Lightest Africa', 'The Sisters' and the comedy 'The Patent Bacillus'. Nobel was familiar with Shakespeare and socialised with Victor Hugo. His bookshelf groaned under works by Selma Lagerlöf, Ibsen, Turgenev and Byron. Naturally, he read everything in the original language. Emile Zola, on the other hand, was held in contempt and called 'a writer of filth'.

But Nobel himself could also descend to crude erotic allusions. His childhood friend, the explosives expert, Alarik Liedbeck, was a confidant and their letters were full of references to women, sexual parts and sexuality: 'By the way, do you have any way of contacting that sweet little governess I saw recently in Vienna, at whose very appearance both mouths water for all men?'

Or: 'Women are quite interesting of course, but even when one can no longer plug their holes, one can plug that of ignorance – and the brain's interest survives the cock's. Amen!'

These are the words of a voluptuary, but Alfred Nobel was at heart a romantic. He stored his letters under 'To and From Men' or 'To and From Women'. It many ways, it was symptomatic that Nobel had only two deep loves, of which one seemed to be merely platonic – with, however, interesting aspects.

Bertha Kinsky was an Austrian aristocrat. In the spring of 1876 she

Bertha Kinsky, later von Suttner, was 33 when the fabulously wealthy bachelor of Avenue Malakoff in Paris hired her as housekeeper-com-secretary in the spring of 1876. Almost 30 years later, she would be given the Nobel Peace Prize for her pacifist novel, Lay Down Your Arms.

noticed a classified advertisement in the 'Neue Freie Presse': 'Very rich, highly educated elder gentleman, resident in Paris, seeks lady of equivalent age, good at languages, as secretary with responsibility for a household.'

She came, but stayed only a week. It was not that the chemistry was wrong between them; back in Vienna, Bertha's fiancé, Arthur von Suttner had developed cold feet and telegraphed: 'Come home and marry me!' He was noticeably jealous. She hesitated; she enjoyed being with the sophisticated Nobel. But rather wife than housekeeper, she reasoned, apologising for her vacillation.

Extraordinarily, Bertha von Suttner was to reappear in Alfred Nobel's chronicle – as a Peace Prize winner. She wrote a book titled 'Down With Weapons!' which created quite a stir in Europe, with researchers arguing over cause and effect in the issue: did he influence her or she him? Or did they influence each other?

There is no question that Alfred Nobel always had peaceful ambitions for his inventions. He never even got into fights as a child; he had a tranquil nature as a teenager and always made it a point of honour to resolve conflicts with arguments. But at a certain stage, he began to ponder deeply on world peace. One of his theories was the Balance of Terror. A dream was to institute an organ or court that would adjudicate on international conflicts. He was in fact anticipating the United Nations.

The other romance was far more destructive.

At Alfred Nobel's death in 1896, the 26-year-old executor of Nobel's will, Ragnar Sohlman, was suddenly faced with a dangerous dilemma 'that threatens to turn me both grey-haired then bald'. A woman named Sofie Hess had sent him a request for a large sum of money. In exchange, she was offering 216 love letters from Alfred Nobel. It was blackmail, plain and simple. Sohlman paid up and many years passed before the letters' content became public. It makes touching, and at times shocking, reading. The couple had met at an Austrian spa, Baden bei Wien, in the summer of 1876. He was hoping for a cure from another of his ailments and she was working in the bakery.

'I'm eighteen,' she told him. In fact, she was 25. For the rest of his life, Alfred Nobel would believe that he was 25 years senior to Sofie Hess, not 18, as was the case. She was a pretty, flirtatious girl. Her

Sofie Hess was one of the few natural forces Alfred Nobel was unable to tame. She was said to be pretty, vulgar, hysterical, loose and far too fond of her drink. Their destructive love story lasted 15 years. Even after Nobel's death, Hess continued to blackmail his estate.

The sumptuous 25-room villa Mio Nido (My Nest) in San Remo. The house was 'characterised by the kind of exoticism imported by Italian officers who had served in North Africa.' It had a temple-like bathing house and a steel jetty that Nobel had built for test firings over the sea.

Next page: The magnificent conservatory that served as living room at 53 Avenue Malakoff in Paris. Alfred Nobel bought the luxury apartment, close to the Arc de Triomphe and the Bois de Boulogne, in 1873. It was here that he composed the famous will founding the Nobel Prize – seen by many as his most important 'invention'.

gaze did not flinch, and her smile was challenging. She was completely uneducated and not exactly the right company for an intellectual man of the world. What would people think? But in his bottomless loneliness, he took her as a lover.

For the first time in his 44 years, Alfred Nobel was as lovesick as a March cat. His first letters were full of phrases such as 'my dear, sweet child', 'my little, beloved thing' and she was obviously flattered. She was not put off by his age – more by his darker side, glimpsed on occasion behind the disciplined façade. Her Swedish lover smiled little.

For his part, Nobel found that she seldom understood what he was talking about. She seemed, actually, quite dumb. He corrected her spelling mistakes, rapping his hand to his forehead as he did. 'She is like a three-year-old in a 30-year-old's body,' he would sigh, struggling like Higgins with an Eliza whose greatest gift appeared to be in bed.

Sofie Hess's posthumous reputation was not flattering. 'She cheated on Nobel with every waiter,' said her sister Amelia, and Alfred Nobel's nephew, Emanuel, wrote that one evening, Sofie seemingly tried to seduce him: 'Oh, it's raining so heavily! You'll have to stay here tonight.' Preserved sales slips indicate that on one occasion she bought 57 bottles of wine and liqueur in a period of 49 days. Talk in the Nobel family was of 'an hysterical gold-digger who treated fine men badly'.

It was typical. Alfred Nobel had tamed the strongest forces in the universe, but before this woman he became week-kneed and gawky.

And he was ashamed of what his friends thought. 'Never leave my letters in the open!' he wrote to her on 6 July 1870 and became nervous when she said she was coming to visit – should he introduce her as his wife or as 'Madame Hess'? 'I no longer know how to behave with educated people,' he complained. 'I don't dare meet them for fear of making a clumsy mistake. And it's your fault, Sofie! Life with you has made me a spiritual cripple.'

He wrote to his sister-in-law Edla, Ludvig's wife: 'What contrasts there are between us! You, surrounded by love, happiness, frolic, pulsating life, caring and cared for, comforting and being comforted, anchored in contentment; me, lurching around, compass- and rudderless like a useless and ill-fated wreck of a life.'

Sofie became pregnant at last, in the autumn of 1890 – but with an Austrian cavalry captain.

The world's first aluminium sailing boat. Alfred Nobel christened his creation 'Mignon' and took her for a maiden voyage on Lake Zurich in 1891. She was a 12-metre boat able to take 30 passengers. The inventor himself is at the helm.

Kapy von Kapyvar was a well-meaning fool and Alfred Nobel was magnanimous. Until the captain sent a begging letter – 'Dear Mr. Nobel! I beg you in God's name not to let us down. Sofie and I are in Reichenghall with no funds at all' – and fell out of favour.

In the last years, many fought over Nobel's money. He noted once that 'the Post Office delivers at least two dozen requests and begging letters a day, for a total of at least 20,000 kronor, which makes at least seven million kronor a year, which leads me to assume that it would be far better to have a poor reputation than to be known as helpful.'

Nobel himself spent only small amounts. He might go to a casino to keep someone company, but would bet only tiny sums. He neither danced nor played any musical instrument. There are reports that he sometimes smoked when nervous but generally, his vices were almost non-existent. Most of what he spent went on travel between health spas and the purchase of a new home, a huge villa in San Remo on the Mediterranean coast. A conflict with the French authorities, eager to lay their hands on his explosives, resulted in Nobel being declared an 'undesirable alien'. In 1894, he also bought Björkborn, a country estate, and the Bofors company, both in the Swedish province of Värmland. With lust and energy, he threw himself into the task of producing cannon for the nation's warships.

In St Petersburg, the Nobels' neighbours were forced to get used to nightly detonations from the brothers' tiny kitchen. San Remo's residents also had reason to complain about repeated explosions, this time from the narrow steel jetty Alfred had built.

In 1887, he had produced the third of his life's great inventions – smokeless gunpowder, or cordite. Riflemen would no longer disappear into a cloud of smoke after their first shot. (And Wild West gunfights would become viable.) Nobel went on experimenting: on a silent gun, a drill powered by compressed air, a moving picture camera, a flying torpedo, a railway carriage on gigantic steel balls and a kind of hi-fi player that reduced unpleasant higher tones. He also had radical ideas for blood transfusions, a child allowance system and old-age pensions. There were plans for synthetic rubber, silk and varnish and synthetic clothing.

He had a wild idea for preventing train crashes through a 'front-rider' – a little, powered trolley a couple of hundred metres ahead of the locomotive, warning the driver via an electric cable if it met

The tragic balloon flight to the North Pole undertaken by Solomon Andrée in 1897 was made possible thanks to Alfred Nobel's generous sponsorship. It was the inventor's idea to include Siberian homing pigeons in the expedition's equipment.

S.A. 16 maj 95.

Hr Andrées nordpolsexpedition.

Nytt storartadt bidrag af dr Alfred Nobel.

Dr Alfred Nobel har höjt sitt e bjudna bidrag för öfveringeniör An drées nordpolsfärd i ballong ända ti 65,000 kronor, d. v. s. hälften af de beräknade kostnaden, med vilkor a den återstående hälften af kostnade inom två månader tecknas från annu håll.

an obstacle. Another idea was a balloon used for photography that would release its pictures by parachute.

When Swedish explorer Salamon Andrée was planning his doomed balloon expedition to the North Pole, Nobel provided some financial backing as well as suggesting that Andrée use a steering sail, draglines and carrier pigeons for sending back reports.

'Pigeons? But they'd freeze to death!' protested Andrée.

'Not Siberian pigeons,' answered Nobel. 'There's lots of pigeons up in northern Russia that have no trouble at all with winter cold, if they're looked after properly. Imagine what a grand reception they would get and how much they could mean for the expedition's safety!'

Among Alfred Nobel's most bizarre brainwaves was his detailed plan for a suicide hotel in Paris. He wanted a tranquil and elegant hospice where guests were treated like kings, exiting this world painlessly. None of the guests would know exactly when their ultimate wish would be fulfilled. At table, one of the glasses used for water or wine would contain a sleeping potion and poison. At the next meal, those still alive would simply note that one of their number had 'moved'.

To Alfred's surprise, the French authorities were less than enthusiastic. It did not help that he explained at length the benefit in not having people 'slit their throats in common, unpleasant places or jumping in the Seine and fouling the water for other citizens'.

He never abandoned his literary ambition. Towards the end of his life, he spent hours in his study rewriting his play, 'Nemesis', set in Rome in the year 1598. His model was Shelley's 'The Cenci' and his theme was the treachery of the Church in departing from 'the true word of Jesus'.

The play was, unfortunately, high-flown rubbish. Nobel tried to shoehorn in his entire philosophy of life and weighed down the script with symbolism and spiritual bric-a-brac. And after all the years abroad his Swedish was hopelessly out of date. After his death, his family burned all the copies they found.

It is also of interest to note that at the end of his life, Alfred Nobel listed a number of subjects that he intended to 'philosophise on', among them:

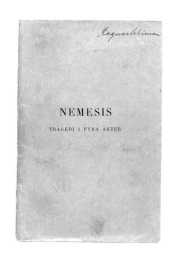

The only known original imprint of Alfred Nobel's ponderous play 'Nemesis'. Shortly after his death, Alfred's family incinerated all the copies they could find.

- cooperative atoms
- the different religions
- a system of government based on a new concept
- the cells and the universe

It is an affectionate list, at odds with his view of himself as 'a valueless instrument of brooding, alone in the world and with darker thoughts than anyone can imagine'.

Also amusing was his private cashbook, which may well have included the greatest contrasts ever seen in a single cash column:

Flowers, Madame R, 40

Coat, 0:25

Remitted Ludvig, 2,300,000.

Was he stingy? No, but careful with money. Relatives and their children were always remembered on holidays and birthdays with beautiful gifts. And he tried to get to Stockholm every September 30 to be with his beloved mother, Andriette. He would do anything for his closest circle of friends – but few passed the entry requirements. 'Believe me, one gathers many friends only among dogs, that you feed with the flesh of others, and among worms, that you feed with your own.'

Nobel's French cook, offered a present for her impending wedding, told him: 'I should like to receive what Monsieur Nobel earns in a single day.' Her request amused him and he spent considerable time working it out before presenting her with a sum so large that she enjoyed interest payments for the rest of her life.

'The richest vagabond in Europe' the press called him, but he was considering moving home to Sweden for good.

He left it too late.

On 7 December 1896, Alfred Nobel suffered a cerebral haemorrhage in his San Remo villa. He died three days later, just as his worst vision had foreshadowed: 'When I die, it will be alone with no loved friend in the room to hold my hand through the struggle and afterwards to close my eyelids – there will be only a lackey, paid for it.'

The shock came when his will was opened. Of the 33 million kronor he had gathered as a private fortune, 31 were earmarked for a special fund that would distribute the interest annually to 'those

The last known picture, taken in 1890, of the 'dynamite plug' who spent a lifetime oscillating between frenetic creativity and pitch-black melancholy. It would be another six years before his death, which indicates how withdrawn, almost painfully shy, his last years were.

who, during the preceding year, shall have conferred the greatest benefit on mankind'.

Not only was his family furious, but the loyal executor, Ragnar Sohlman, realised that the French authorities could at any time get a whiff of considerable inheritance taxes. How could he quickly get the 33 million back to Sweden without attracting attention?

Young Sohlman acted with exceptional speed and vision. Sitting on the coachbox with a loaded revolver in his hand as his covered coach made its way through the streets of Paris, he transported Nobel's fortune from its secret safety deposit box to the Swedish consulate. There, the money was wrapped in small packages – each worth about two million kronor – and sent off as ordinary, discreet mail to Sweden. To the end, Alfred Nobel played the main role in an international thriller, full of intrigue and drama and with enormous consequences. Among the actors was the Swedish king, Oscar II, who regarded the will as 'unpatriotic' and tried in vain to have the annual donation reserved for Swedish citizens only: 'It is as though a woman had thought all this up!'

The Nobel Prize was distributed for the first time on 10 December 1901 – exactly five years after Alfred's death. Of all the genius's ideas, his Prize is probably the 'invention' with the greatest force, more than all those sticks of dynamite.

One hundred years later, the shockwave is still being felt across the face of the earth.

The will that infuriated the Swedish King – but which today remunerates masterminds across the world. The document carried detailed instructions on how to take care of its author's dead body: the arteries were to be opened and the corpse to be cremated. Like his father, Alfred Nobel had a deep fear of being buried alive.

No 73. År 1897 den 5 Februari uppvist vid vittnesförhör inför
Stockholms Rådstufvurätts sjette Afdelning; betyga
Lösen En krona   ex officio.
   aut. å prot.   Jacob Kinders.

Testament

Jag undertecknad Alfred Bernhard
Nobel förklarar härmed efter moget
betänkande min yttersta vilja i afseende
å den egendom jag vid min död kan ef-
terlemna vara följande:

Mina Brorssöner Hjalmar och Ludvig
Nobel, söner af min Broder Robert Nobel, erhålla
hvardera en summa af Två Hundra Tusen Kronor;

Min Brorsson Emanuel Nobel erhåller Fyra
Hundra Tusen och min Brorsdotter Mina Nobel
Ett Hundra Tusen Kronor;

Min Broder Robert Nobels döttrar Ingeborg
och Tyra erhålla hvardera Ett Hundra Tusen Kronor;

Fröken Olga Boettger, för närvarande boende
hos Fru Brand, 10 Rue St Florentin i Paris, erhåller
Ett Hundra Tusen Francs;

Fru Sofie Kapy von Kapivar, hvars adress
är känd af Anglo-Oesterreichische Bank i Wien,
är berättigad till en lifränta af 6000 Floriner Ö.W.
som betalas henne af bagde Bank och hvarföre jag
i denna Bank deponerat 150,000 Fl. Ungerska Statspapper.

Herr Alarik Liedbeck, boende 26 Sturegatan,
Stockholm, erhåller Ett Hundra Tusen Kronor;

Fröken Elise Antun, boende 32 Rue de Lübeck,
Paris, är berättigad till en lifränta af Två Tusen
Fem Hundra Francs. Dessutom innestår hos mig
för närvarande Tyratis åtta Tusen Francs henne till-
hörigt kapital som äges att till henne återbetalas;

Herr Alfred Hammond, Waterford, Texas,
United States, erhåller Tio Tusen Dollars;

Fröknarne Emmy Winkelmann och Marie Win-

1894 den 30 September, å hvilka hänförsig en senare
Dess testamente, för hvilken Alfred Nobels dessförinnan
i detta förklarade förtestamente, samt denna verifikation
protokollet förvalas, betyga på en gång samtidigt på sätt?
                                        Christian Reg...

The first Nobel Prize ceremony on 10 December 1901. Wilhelm Conrad Roentgen is being presented with his prize money by King Oscar: 150,000 kronor (c. $18,000) – an incredible amount for the time. The place was the Royal Academy of Music in Stockholm, the only premises large enough to accommodate so many prominent guests. Paradoxically, Alfred Nobel himself despised honorary degrees, medals and 'such tinsel'.

THE SPIRITIST

Baltzar von Platen 1898–1984

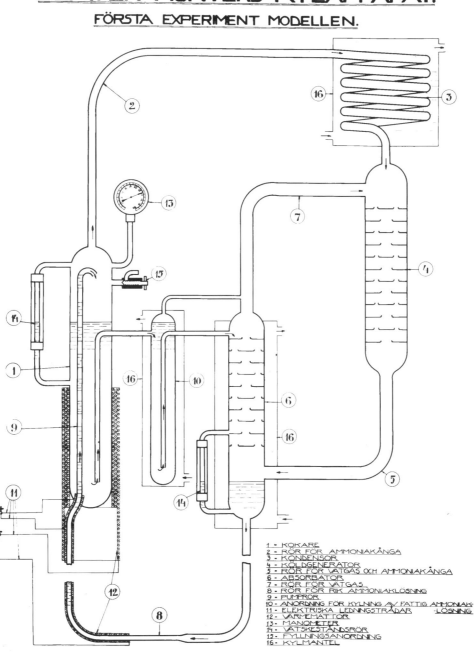

PLATEN-MUNTERS KYLAPPAPAT.

FÖRSTA EXPERIMENT MODELLEN.

1 - KOKARE
2 - RÖR FÖR AMMONIAKÅNGA
3 - KONDENSOR
4 - KÖLDGENERATOR
5 - RÖR FÖR VÄTGAS OCH AMMONIAKÅNGA
6 - ABSORBATOR
7 - RÖR FÖR VÄTGAS
8 - RÖR FÖR RIK AMMONIAKLÖSNING
9 - PUMPRÖR
10 - ANORDNING FÖR KYLNING AV FATTIG AMMONIAK-
11 - ELEKTRISKA LEDNINGSTRÅDAR   -LÖSNING
12 - VÄRMEMATTOR
13 - MANOMETER
14 - VÄTSKESTÅNDSRÖR
15 - FYLLNINGSANORDNING
16 - KYLMANTEL

In the autumn of 1960, Swedish newspapers mounted a feverish hunt for 'a gentleman from Ronneby, 30-40 years of age, of medium height and normal build'. The hunt had begun when a 62-year-old inventor, Baltzar von Platen, had placed an advertisement in a paper, pleading for help.

On an express train, southbound for Frankfurt am Main on 21 September, he had shared a compartment with a man from Ronneby. Also in the compartment was a German woman of about 25, with whom von Platen had discussed in some depth the English novel 'Ships that Meet in the Night'. Her suitcase and von Platen's folded overcoat were on the same overhead luggage rack. In the pocket of his coat was a folded paper 'of enormous importance'. Could the document have been taken by mistake along with the suitcase? Did the man from Ronneby perhaps know the woman's identity?

What did von Platen mean by 'of enormous importance'? asked a reporter.

Baltzar von Platen replied that he could not provide a complete answer to the question. All he would say was that the document contained four points germane to a new invention that could change the way the world worked. A real sensation.

The inventor was asked whether he suspected foul play.

'No,' he answered, 'But I'm worried about what will happen if the paper falls into the wrong hands.' His reply aroused more consternation than the original advertisement. Few suspected that what von Platen had scribbled on the piece of paper was nothing less than the Holy Grail of all inventors: a perpetual motion machine. The solution had come to him on the morning of Christmas Eve 1914, through a spirit being. He was 16 at the time. 'I understood it to be an intelligent being from another planet. I spent the whole day in a trance. I couldn't even get to church at five o'clock to hear Salomon Smith's excellent baritone in Silent Night.'

All his life, von Platen would cling to the prophesy of perpetual motion. Everything he invented – the refrigerator, artificial diamonds, the dripless tap, and improvements to the producer-gas generator – was a by-product of his quest. And just as he was in a position to change the world, the plans disappeared on a German express train.

It sounds like the plot of a cheap novel, but in many ways it was a typical incident in a life characterised from start to finish by bizarre

A mind in constant movement – at times to the point of over-boil – created our modern refrigerator. Baltzar von Platen (1898-1984) fluctuated between ingenuity and off-the-wall brainstorms. This was amply shown in the amazing story of "A Gentleman from Ronneby", from a 1960s newspaper.

Previous page: One of the first sketches of the world's first refrigerator without moving parts. All his life, Baltzar von Platen would claim that a spirit being who appeared on Christmas Eve of 1914 revealed how to capture and use the heat loss resulting from the formation of steam.

episodes and thick headlines. In 1907, Baltzar von Platen, the young son of a magistrate in Ystad on the southern Swedish coast, came rushing home to ask for pad and paper to write a letter: 'To His Majesty the King. I am a nine-year-old schoolboy at Ystad Grammar School. Today a boy was nearly murdered by his headmaster. I shouted "you hooligan!" to the headmaster and then ran home. So I shall shortly be murdered. Your Majesty is the only one who can save me. Your Majesty's humble servant, Baltzar von Platen.'

Always hunted, always hyped. Always enlivened by new, ingenious ideas, always terrified that someone else will get there first, steal the ideas or simply steal his glory. Among Swedish inventors, Baltzar von Platen is the most colourful, the most controversial and the most ridiculed. But also one of the smartest. Without his brains, Sweden's beloved ice-cold 'punsch' liqueur would be drunk lukewarm and taps would keep Swedes awake at night with irritating dripping. Without him, the history of science in Sweden would have far fewer entertaining stories and audacious leaps of knowledge.

Baltzar von Platen was like no one else. This was plain from his childhood in the family's prosperous home in Ystad. When only five, he questioned his mother's statement that the body becomes dust after death, saying: 'Impossible. That would mean the earth was growing all the time!'

His mother, Ingeborg, was a good pianist and an amateur painter. His father, Philip, was an imposing man, from a military family background. Left half-deaf from an attack of scarlet fever as a child, Philip von Platen was forced to give up his dream of an army career and become a magistrate instead. He put the fear of God in people with his booming voice and his imposing stature, but was secretly a pussycat. There were four children; Baltzar was his only son, and a true pain in the neck. As a child, Baltzar was forever asking questions. Philip's motto was 'Honour before all,' but one day he heard his son singing rebelliously, 'I am tired of honour. Long live happiness!' so loudly that the walls shook in the von Platen mansion.

'What are you singing?' thundered father.

'Nothing. Just what it says in Verdi's "La forza del destino".'

There is no such line in 'La forza del destino', but the boy had a quicker tongue than most.

In a biology lesson in primary school, given by the headmaster,

He exasperated his teachers by continually questioning accepted theories and by presenting his own mathematical theorems. Someone who had already talked to spirits at the age of 16 perhaps had little to fear …

A precocious seven-year-old. Young Baltzar delved early into the mysteries of the universe and death. He was good at thinking, singing, inventing – and lying.

Baltzar was asked for the Latin name for a flower spotted in a ditch. Baltzar gave no answer. 'Do you not know?' asked the headmaster. 'Yes,' replied the boy, 'I'm just wondering how the small leaves up at the top of those trees can suck up water from the ground. It's ten metres at least.'

It was perhaps no wonder that a pupil like that divided the teachers into two camps. One appreciated the freethinker; the other felt he threatened them and the rules.

Baltzar von Platen often quoted from Winston Churchill's autobiography, 'My Early Life', in which the statesman wrote that he was continually dismissed as 'a stupid donkey'. Little Baltzar was subject to the same kind of opposition, not least from the brutal headmaster, known derisively as 'Snuff', who delighted in punishing insubordinate small boys.

There was also 'dishonest Mr Beer' and the 'evil Professor Monkey', so it was scarcely surprising that the young von Platen sought another life in day-dreams and on the wide beaches of Falsterbo during summer holidays. (The family was among the first to buy a summer cottage on 'Sweden's Riviera'.) In memoirs published in 1974, von Platen recounted how, as an eleven-year-old, he had built a raft, then saved a thirteen-year-old friend from drowning when the friend's hand had caught in the anchor.

When he was twelve, young Baltzar built a 'sailing wagon' – a kind of land yacht – that veered wildly, flattening the neighbour's fence with its heavy, oak hull. The next year, he built a sleek sailing canoe and sashayed along the coastline, singing famous operatic arias that he had learnt from the gramophone.

He really would have preferred to be an opera singer. He was immensely devoted to music. But when the family maid, Ebba Olsson, yelled at him from the shore to be careful with his voice 'until you are past puberty!' he shut right up. He needed to preserve his talents for greater occasions. But spirit beings intervened.

This was pure Baltzar von Platen. Just as for his compatriot, the savant-theologian Emanuel Swedenborg, there would be a lifelong tussle between the exactitude of the natural sciences and the heavenliness of the hereafter. Others may choose between logic and emotion; von Platen chose both. He was both realist and dreamer. He saw no contradiction at all between inventing the refrigerator and speaking

Diamonds may be a girl's best friend, but the refrigerator was still Baltzar von Platen's most appreciated invention. The advertisement is from the 1950s, when the average volume of a Swedish refrigerator was 80 litres. Today it is 300.

A run of mild winters around 1920 produced an ice shortage in the entire Western world and hastened the development of the refrigerator. Financier Axel Wallen-Gren, who had made a fortune with the vacuum cleaner, produced the first Electrolux refrigerator in 1921. The actual cooling unit was in a 'backpack' at the rear.

with ghosts. This may have been his greatness. When others shut down their thought processes, crying 'Impossible!' Baltzar von Platen rode on. Like a Copernicus or a Columbus, he disdained what might be thought possible or impossible. He challenged education, challenged even the laws of nature. When his maths teacher wrote out the famous equation 'Distance equals speed multiplied by time', he protested loudly.

'I don't understand! How can speed be distant?' Which, of course, led to yet another fail mark, and to extra lessons. These were given by a friendly young graduate student who lived in a haunted house. The result was that the maths lessons were mixed with spooky stories about the ethereal guest – apparently a manservant who had salvaged the captain's money chest from a frigate stranded off the coast and was murdered for it by his greedy master.

When he began studies at Lund University in 1917, von Platen was a wizard of a boy and very highly strung. Not long afterwards, his old playmate from Falsterbo, the one who almost drowned, was killed in an air attack on a field hospital in Germany. When a female friend took ill during their visit to an opera performance and died shortly afterwards, the 19-year-old Baltzar suspected that spirits were at work. Hadn't he been lax in building their perpetual motion machine, even though the spirit beings had so clearly drawn the plans for him in his head?

This background might help in judging his behaviour when he sat an oral examination by Professor Manne Siegbahn, a Nobel Prize winner.

'Prove the Carnot Cycle!' challenged the professor.

'I was both surprised and happy,' remembered Baltzar von Platen in his memoirs, 'since only three years previously, I had discovered the enormously simple, graphic proof of this equation. So simple that my mother's seamstress Olga could learn it.'

It took von Platen four seconds to draw the four lines on a piece of paper. But the professor was far from pleased. He had never seen the graphic proof and demanded that the student prove it the way Carnot had. Discussion became vociferous argument, ending with Baltzar von Platen shouting: 'I shall never waste even ten seconds in learning Carnot's equation by heart! Especially since Carnot's father murdered Louis XVI and his consort, Marie-Antoinette!'

Finally tiring of a dripping tap, von Platen went to his drawing board to think. 'What was it I learned about high pressure when I was working on synthetic diamonds?' There were connections between all of von Platen's inventions. The picture from his office is from 1960.

As he stormed out into the corridor, he shouted 'Marie-Antoinette!' loud enough to be heard all the way to the dean's office.

It was around this time that Baltzar von Platen was tempted to become a priest. 'But you're so often such a nasty person!' his mother let slip.

'Yes, but there would be plenty of time left for inventing.'

The choice actually came down to a matter of seconds. As a 20-year-old, Baltzar von Platen was journeying by train north to Stockholm to commence studies at the Royal Institute of Technology, but almost got off the train at the university town of Lund, only a few kilometres from his starting point. 'I'll enter the theological faculty here instead,' he thought. 'I've decided: I'll become a priest.' But as he went to get off, the train started moving again. Once at his original destination, and outside the dean's door at the Institute, he again doubted his choice; he considered telling Dean Magnell that he had become ill and would have to return home.

In his old age, von Platen would at times regret not acting on that impulse. Life as an inventor was often painful and chaotic. 'A pity that I did not become a cavalry officer or priest. So much trouble would have been avoided!' But spirits have a way of toying with the fate of humans.

Baltzar von Platen would no longer risk the opprobrium of examiners; he had finally found teachers who could glimpse his genius. One of them was later to become the technical manager of Separator, the company now known as Alfa Laval. The teacher wanted to given von Platen top marks for an oral exam, but von Platen protested: 'Oh no! I have never been interested in grades. Mark me as passed – that'll do!'

Was he a bogus?

Perhaps. It is not easy to sit in judgement on this multi-faceted personality. If you study his diploma carefully, you will find a strange annotation. At the subject for which he was given merely a pass grade, von Platen had printed: 'With my left hand on the Bible at John III, verse 16, and with my right hand holding my pen, I hereby swear that the examining teacher awarded me a higher grade, but I refused it.'

Shy, self-confident, magnanimous, demanding, irritable, humble, belligerent, contrite, spiritual, rational – all epithets are equally accurate. His universal genius was still unreleased, oscillating him between hot and cold.

At the age of 64, Baltzar von Platen poses in front of a mural in his 17th-century Stockholm mansion. It was here that he made most of his discoveries, among them the synthetic diamond after blowing up numerous beer-can-sized pressure chambers in his basement.

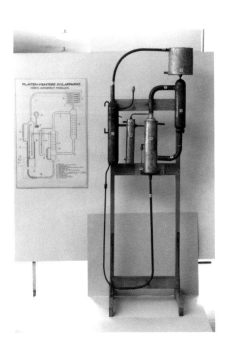

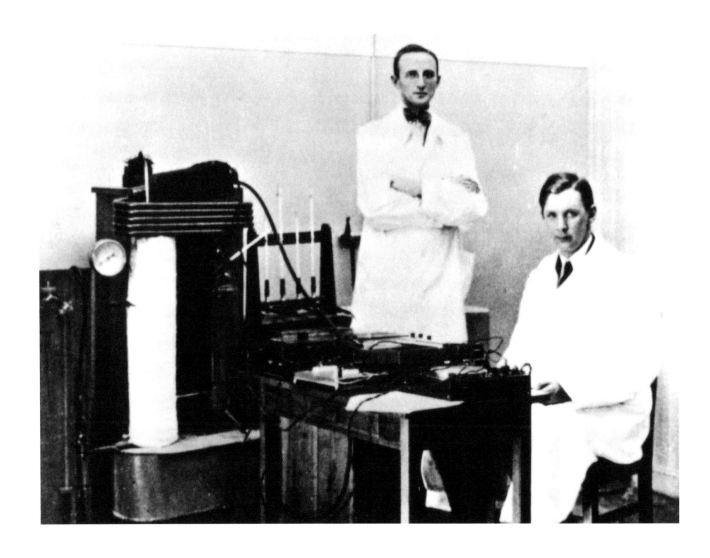

Just like the basic principle of that machine for perpetual motion in the spirit's prophecy of Christmas Eve, 1914: 'You know there is a world war. You know there will be fuel shortages. So construct a machine that extracts heat from cold surroundings, raises the temperature and spreads heat to our living quarters.'

Less than a century later, this would become known as the thermal heat generator, but what Baltzar von Platen did was to create its opposite.

Meanwhile, his attention had been caught by a fellow student at the Institute. Carl Munters was hard to ignore. Rumour had it that he had invented an automobile to finance his studies. For three years, the southerner observed the Stockholmer. 'There's a genius I could never be friends with,' thought von Platen. They found themselves seated beside each other at a lunch break. Munters began talking about his latest invention, an automatic shutter release for a camera. Baltzar von Platen listened politely, and then suggested an improvement. Carl Munters was visibly upset.

'Why are you angry with me?' asked von Platen later.

'I'm not angry with you, but at myself, because I was explaining my invention to someone who didn't need the explanation. I don't often meet people like that.'

It was the beginning of an intensive friendship. Most evenings at half past nine they would shut themselves up in a rented apartment to work, stumbling into bed at half past four the next morning. They began every work session with tea and cake laced with liqueur. They skipped morning classes, spending just enough time and energy in afternoon classes to earn a pass grade.

Egged on by Carl's father, Anders Munters, the youths attacked the problem of 'making a refrigeration device without moving parts, in which one extremity becomes cold when the other is heated.'

It took a month and two days to prepare the first prototype. It easily maintained minus 40 degrees Celsius, but was far too big and clumsy for use in the home. Their next refrigerator was better sized, but their chief sponsor, Hugo Tillquist, a wholesaler and gentleman who took care of all the bills and was going to help 'the boys' sell their thingamajig, wanted further refinements. He promised to handle all contacts with companies that might be interested. Gustaf de Laval's Separator Co. was a prospective customer, but the price – a million kronor

The first Platen–Munter prototype hardly resembled what we know as a refrigerator. But the basic principle is still in use, especially for refrigeration in places without access to electricity. Briefly, the idea was that heat is used up in turning liquid into gas and that heat can be extracted from air in the refrigerator, which thereby cools.

It began with mistrustful glances at each other across the lecture hall. Later, they rented a two-room office in Stockholm where they ate cake, drank tea and arranged for the Swedish population to have reliable access to ice to chill their 'punsch' liqueur. The refrigerator was the prodigies' prodigious research accomplishment for their degree. Baltzar von Platen (arms crossed) and Carl Munters needed little more than a month to produce it.

Next page: ghost world. The aging Baltzar von Platen among sketches and blueprints for his perpetual motion machine and the manuscript for his autobiography, 'Spirits and the Perpetuum Mobile'. Seldom has there been anyone as smart, as colourful and as ridiculed.

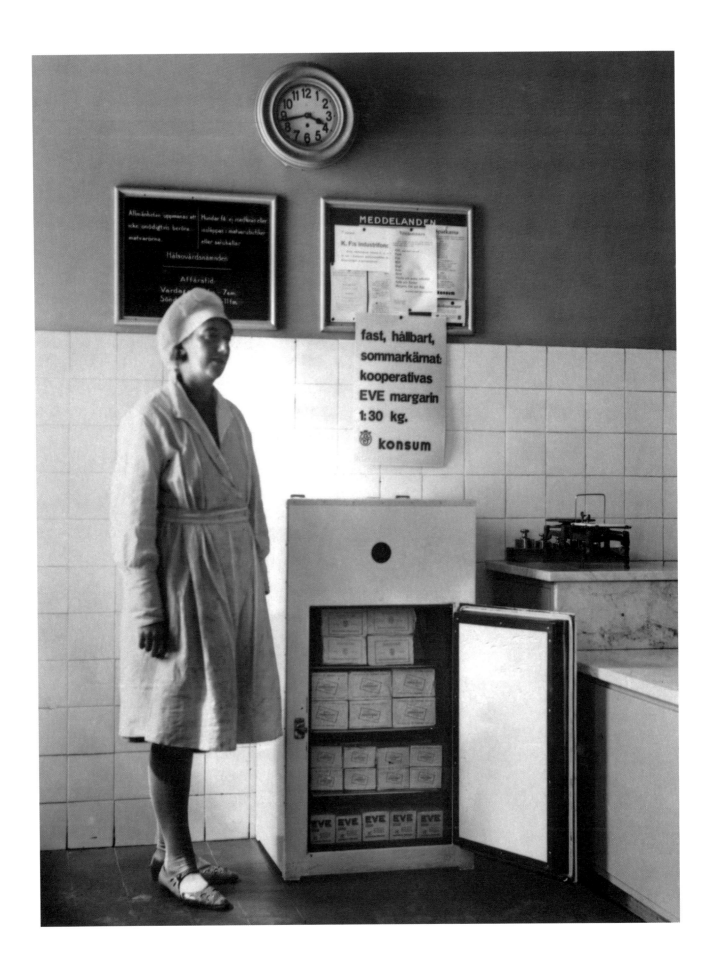

(approx. $100,000) – provoked the company's technical manager, Erik Forsberg, to rage.

Tillquist answered: 'A million is nothing! It's no more than Munters, von Platen and I spend on lunch!'

This gross exaggeration offended Forsberg. He was by coincidence the examiner to whom Baltzar von Platen had said, 'Mark me as passed – that'll do.' And now the boy wanted a million kronor! 'No, my young friend, we won't be doing business together.'

Baltzar von Platen came up with another prospect to approach: Johnny Walker, the whisky king. Walker was a distant relative on von Platen's mother's side. He must need ice for his drinks, reasoned von Platen. A bout of influenza with complications ruined the scheme, however. Recovering after two months of illness, he found that Tillquist and Munters had already signed a contract. 'For chicken feed!' growled von Platen. 'There goes a fortune for us three.'

In his autobiography, von Platen devoted page after page to stories of how businessmen tried to cheat him. Among his enemies was Ernst Aurell, the Chief Executive Officer of Electrolux, who was quoted in 1927 as saying: 'I have watched with pity and amusement von Platen's attempts to improve the performance of Electrolux's refrigerator.'

Von Platen answered: 'The pity you feel for me is only a fraction of the pity I feel for [Electrolux founder] Director Axel Wenner-Gren for the damage he has incurred, having you as CEO.'

The executive turned red, then white. He opened a drawer in his desk, convincing Baltzar that he was reaching for a pistol. Baltzar leapt forward and laughed loudly, right in the CEO's ear.

'I knew how to laugh that way because I had been practising Iago's aria from the Verdi 'Otello'. Many singers end it with that kind of laugh.'

The words were those of a misunderstood, volatile genius. Baltzar von Platen often appeared obsessive, tilting at the windmills of the powerful. He ought to have been happy that, in Germany, a certain Albert Einstein was said to be impressed with the cocky young Swedes' invention. Instead, repetitious quarrels over royalties, suggestions for improvements and whether the refrigerators would be gas- or electricity-driven would cast deep shadows over his life. Especially after 102 people died in the United States because of a construction fault – over von Platen's protests, the Americans had insisted that the

Chill out! The refrigerator was one of many symbols for the emerging Swedish welfare state. Meanwhile, the inventor himself was ensconced in his posh villa in southern Skåne province, tackling the eternal mysteries.

refrigerators be powered by coal gas – he became bitter and resigned. He almost suffered a similar fate: for two years, von Platen suffered from chronic headaches when at home, until a female dinner guest sniffed the air and remarked: 'My dear Baltzar, isn't that gas?'

Constantly in danger, constantly cheated, constantly at a crossroads, always hot on the trail of a Great Secret: Baltzar von Platen's life was a spine-tingling novel, a juicy tale with a labyrinthine plot where the truth is sometimes elusive.

One minute he was trying to prove that the rich and famous Swedish painter, Anders Zorn, was the illegitimate son of a certain Count Louis Wrede, and thus related to Baltzar von Platen himself. The next, he was preparing to release a gramophone record with a spoken message: 'You are not stupid. People simply perceive original-ity as stupidity. You are not stupid.' The idea was for the purchaser to play the record every evening at bedtime, with the words repeated until they faded to a whisper. Von Platen was no stranger to the recording studio; since childhood, he had dreamt of being a singer. Now, bitter and disillusioned in the aftermath of another shipwrecked invention, he was strongly considering ditching science for the arts. In 1920, he had holidayed in Venice and had almost 'been thrown into the canal by the enormous sound wave from a human voice'. The voice belonged to Titta Ruffo, one of the great baritones of the day, who happened to be on a passing gondola. 'He thought it a wonderful place to practise his fortissimo.' The two men became acquainted, resulting in an impulsive promise by an animated von Platen to write a book about singing. He was good to his word, launching the theory that true singing comes about when the least possible effort is exerted. 'Anne and the Demiurge' was never pub-lished, but is yet another example of his idea overflow.

Baltzar von Platen could indeed sing. He made a total of eight recordings at Stockholm's Konserthuset hall.

He continued to flirt with spiritualism as well. 'I am no spiritualist,' he asserted, but was fascinated by mediums who could see the past and predict the future. Was time perhaps not linear at all? he won-dered. Was it simply 'a symptom', a murky reflection of a reality still hidden from us humans? Could telepathy become the communica-tions tool of the future? Imagine if we could reach the moon without rockets, using only the power of thought!

The wood-gas or producer-gas car kept Sweden mobile during the Second World War. Baltzar von Platen thought up the idea while sailing home from London on board a cargo ship in 1940.

In 1940, Baltzar von Platen found himself stranded in London; the plane he was booked on had crashed in the sea on its way south from Perth in Scotland. At the Swedish embassy, he ran into a famous Swedish aviator, Count Carl Gustaf von Rosen. The two men liked each other immediately. In what might seem a death wish, they hitched a ride on a cargo ship bound for Finland with 3,000 tonnes of ammunition. Everything went well, however, and the two spent many hours on deck opining on the long-term effects of the war.

Listening to von Rosen gave von Platen an eerie feeling. The count was concerned that fuel was scarce with winter approaching. When he heard that von Platen had constructed a generator that could replace petrol, he pricked up his ears.

'You can power a car with ordinary firewood? How does that work?'

'Simple,' replied von Platen and explained the principle of a producer-gas generator. 'It's nothing new.'

'Maybe not,' replied von Rosen. 'But now, during a lengthy war, is when it will have its breakthrough.'

Baltzar von Platen's ideal mixture of air and gas did in fact keep Sweden mobile during the war, but even here, it was as though the invention did not really matter. It was the same with the dripless tap or artificial diamonds – it was as though he looked up for a minute from his work on perpetual motion, jotted down a few hasty formulas and then returned to his real mission.

The tap took ten minutes to make, he noted laconically: 'I was lying on my bed one day, irritated at a drip in the kitchen. The solution was to combine stainless steel and synthetic rubber. The diamonds? Well, they took a little longer. But I understood the principle as early as Christmas, 1930. The problem was to construct a box that could withstand the enormous pressure needed to crystallise the coal. A car tyre has a pressure of two atmospheres and the deepest ocean trough 1,200 atmospheres. To create diamonds, you need a pressure of 60,000. My solution in the end was twisted piano-wire. Everyone says that I invented artificial diamonds: it's true; they were made in a machine I invented and that I owned. But I didn't make any; it was too expensive. Asea made them on 16 February 1953.'

At this stage, the drama became farce. The race to produce artificial diamonds had all the ingredients of a thriller: nightly experiments in a 17th-century mansion on Stockholm's Southside; pressure chambers the size of beer cans exploding one after the other; litigation against the US firm General Electric which also claimed the idea.

And the upshot: the Swedish diamond industry relocated to a little factory facility in Ystad and the years passing with no tangible result.

He granted his last interview in April 1975. The accompanying photograph showed a birdlike old man with chalk-white hair posing amidst the heavy, opulent furniture of his childhood home in Ystad. The kid had come home. At his feet lay Lasse, a 14-year-old black poodle fond of a scratch on the back. Baltzar had been through two marriages and had fathered two daughters. Now he was living with his sister, Lill, hovering somewhere among the sumptuous furnishings of the mansion. 'I never became rich, I was cheated constantly,' became one of von Platen's lifelong maxims. The truth was that he made about $100,000 from the refrigerator and was well paid for his tap, producer-gas generator and diamonds.

Every day, he would lunch and dine at the home of his private secretary of 25 years' standing. In von Platen's own dining-room was a family tree graphic: on a small branch out to one side was Baltzar von Platen's namesake, a controversial engineer who built the Göta Canal, linking the Baltic and the North Sea. 'Everyone who tries to challenge accepted laws of nature meets derision,' commented von Platen with pride.

Neighbours described von Platen as a friendly but unpractical man. He seemed unable to change an ordinary lock and raised eyebrows by wandering around in his garden at the height of summer so wrapped in clothing that only his nose was visible. He preferred Rome, with its warmer climate.

'But I'm not afraid of growing old. You see, I don't believe in time; I don't believe it exists.'

Almost 80 years of age he was still making headlines. In the middle of the Oil Crisis, a Swedish tabloid ran the news: 'Cars That Run on Air!' followed swiftly by: 'Volvo's Electric Car Ready This Year' and: 'Volvo Tops Stock Market'. It was nothing less than a world sensation. Newspapers called the invention 'one of the 20th century's greatest advances in peaceful technology'. The principle had been known since the 16th century: splitting a metal ring and heating one half will produce electricity from the metal. The Russians have been making 'batteries' this way for years, using heat from kerosene lamps to heat

Great mind at work. Over 80 years old, Baltzar von Platen was still inviting journalists to visit him at his grand home in Ystad. To the end, he was provocative and captivating. Among his more bizarre theories was a method of travelling to the moon using telepathetic power.

the 'battery', producing enough electricity to run a radio set. What no one understood was how von Platen had managed to increase the effect enough to power a car. It appeared difficult though not impossible.

His friends realised that it was von Platen's old perpetual motion machine once again. All his life, von Platen had believed he could produce energy virtually from thin air, by allowing fluids – chiefly ammonia – to vaporise and flow between hot and cold containers. Experts said it was impossible, that this defied the second proposition of thermodynamics: that heat cannot arise from an absence of heat.

Is that so, replied Baltzar von Platen. Then what about the Universe? The birth of new stars? And then, with a characteristic, crushing comment: 'Two kinds of people dismiss my invention: those who have not read my dissertation, and those who read it badly.'

The Royal Patent Office was among the latter; after lengthy deliberation it issued a curt refusal: 'The description does not convincingly prove that the proposed "perpetual motion" effect is delivered.'

Baltzar von Platen announced to the press that he had test-driven the new electric vehicle and that it 'performed perfectly'.

'Can you really get the same power as with the combustion engine?' someone asked.

'No. More, of course! There wouldn't be any point otherwise.'

But the car was never unveiled. In theory, a car might be powered using heated metal rings, but more money was needed, more time, more experiments.

It was well known that von Platen himself was a terrible driver. The entire neighbourhood would take cover whenever he backed his Rover out into the street. It took months for him to master Sweden's 1967 change-over from driving on the left to driving on the right. For the old codger to be in command of a car that wouldn't stop was not a cheering thought. As a person, he was charming, but as an inventor, he was archetypal: eccentric, confused and absent-minded.

Years after the event, there was clarification about the document lost on the train.

The conclusion was also typical for a von Platen episode: what turned up in a coat pocket half a year after the incident if not a folded paper napkin with a few lines jotted on it?

The genius's last move produced fat headlines in the spring of 1975: AIR-POWERED CAR HERE! But the world would wait in vain. But von Platen claimed to have test-driven the car the previous year. 'And it worked perfectly.'

von Platens nya uppfinning en revolution:

BILAR DRIVS MED LUFT!

Evighetsmaskiner med vanlig luft som enda bränsle!

Det är grundprincipen för en helt ny, revolutionerande process som kan göra kärnkraften överflödig.

Metoden ska inom kort patentsökas av den svenske uppfinnaren Baltzar von Platen, 77, avslöjar Svenska Dagbladet.

Ett arabland uppges vara villigt att finansiera projektet med oljepengar.

— Jag tror mig ha funnit villkor som gör det möjligt att konstruera evighetsmaskiner, perpetuum mobile av andra ordningen, säger Baltzar von Platen till SvD.

Risken är stor att svensk industri går miste om de enorma möjligheter som öppnar sig, därför att uppfinnargeniet anser sig tidigare ha blivit illa behandlad av vårt näringsliv, skriver SvD.

— Mänskligheten kommer att få en outtömlig helt miljöofarlig energikälla, om de principer jag utvecklar håller vad de lovar, säger Baltzar von Platen.

Projektet beräknas kosta 40

som gör en evighetsmaskin möjlig.

— Han har bevisat att han är en av vår tids stora uppfinnare. Och han har sysslat med detta problem i 50 år. Alla de uppfinningar han under tiden gjort har egentligen endast varit sidoeffekter av hans idéer om perpetuum mobile av andra ordningen.

Förre chefen för Ingenjörsvetenskapsakademin professor Sven Brohult:

● *Expressen avslöjade i maj 1973 Baltzar von Platens hemliga experiment med Volvos elbil. Är den nya uppfinningen en utveckling av den satsningen?*

Geniet som blev kuggat i fysik...

Av ARNE REBERG

In his agitation, he remembered the 'document' as a sheet of paper, not a simple napkin grabbed at a dinner party. On the train, he had run his hands over his pockets, and not hearing the typical rustling of paper, assumed that the document had fallen out. When it was time to have the coat dry-cleaned, the missing napkin turned up.

This was embarrassing, but also another sign that the spirits were still active. Evil spirits made a vital document disappear in a coat's fold; good spirits hastened a visit to the dry-cleaner's. Evil spirits whispered lies in the ears of Patent Office personnel, while the good ones knew that perpetual motion really existed, and that his life's dream had borne fruit. With stoic calm, he accepted that the world would never understand.

All in all, it was a satisfied 86-year-old who departed this mortal coil in 1984, headed for a new mission. The true adventure was about to begin, he seemed to be thinking. And almost in exhilaration he stepped across the great divide, hopeful to enter a time dimension better suited to his tastes.

Admirers and detractors crowded the road to his grave. His posthumous reputation was mixed. Everyone agreed that it would be a long time before Sweden saw his equal.

At least an eternity.

He saw death as a fascinating journey. Even though most of Baltzar von Platen's inventions were extremely logical, he never really abandoned the shadowy, mysterious world of metaphysics. A kindred spirit of the Swedish mystic, Swedenborg, von Platen passed on in 1984.

LINE IN WATER

Gideon Sundbäck 1880–1954

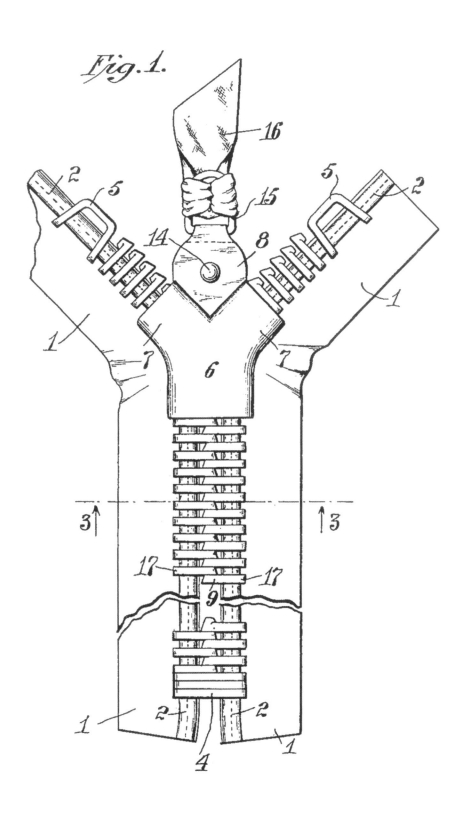

Fig. 1.

The only interest shown in the first zippers came from a few toy manufacturers and a lone magician who thought it would be a great gimmick to have rabbits pop up when he tugged on a metal rod.

Seldom has anything with such a speedy name had such a sluggish start.

If you dig into the ancient history of zips, you discover a diminutive, inventive sewing-machine maker called Elias Howe, who in 1851 put together a complicated construction of hooks and eyes and metal wires, fastened to a leather strip and which, helped by a little 'runner', could be opened and closed.

Not that it was entirely dependable.

In the middle of a ball, a Sunday constitutional or a formal dinner, the lock might suddenly open with an annoying rattle, putting its owner in an embarrassing situation. The slider was not even attached to the lock and was carried separately. The first zippers had sharp catches and dangerous hooks and were reminiscent of mediaeval torture instruments. Weathering her strong protests, Howe finally talked his wife into using his 'continuous clothing closure'. So naturally, a catastrophe did occur at a ladies' dinner. A furious Mrs Howe forced her husband to stuff his invention deep in a drawer and vow to dedicate the rest of his career to the more reliable sewing-machine.

Gideon Sundbäck, originally from the southern Swedish province of Småland, reacted in much the same way.

He had been in the United States for two years, struggling to make ends meet at a variety of dead-end jobs. He was probably wondering whatever happened to his dream of America. But when his future and his fortune come knocking in 1907 in the form of a letter from the Universal Fastener Company, Sundbäck was obstinate and unwilling.

'You can offer as much as you want. I am an electrical engineer and an expert on dynamos, not a stupid button-maker!'

But the letter-writer did not give up easily.

His name was Lewis Walker and he was gripped by an obsession. 'Mr Sundbäck' and he would change the world. Together, they would solve a riddle that had baffled mankind through the ages.

Well, at least since 2 October 1891 – a vexing morning for the temporarily accident-prone Whitcomb L. Judson in the town of Meadville, Pennsylvania.

He was desperate not to be merely 'a damn button-maker' but went down in history as the man who found the quickest way to fasten a man's trousers. Gideon Sundbäck (1880–1954) was an electronics engineer from Småland in southern Sweden who travelled to the United States and reluctantly became a famous inventor in the wrong branch.

Previous page: Gideon Sundbäck's own drawing of the zip fastener that would sweep the world, thanks to American servicemen.

The sleepy Judson, late for work, first broke a shoelace then found two loose buttons on his vest. And at that moment, his 19-year-old wife, Elisabeth, shouted for his help: the ties on her corset had snapped.

Mornings like those make history.

Fuming, Judson set off to his job at a bank with flapping vest and shoelaces knotted in several places; he would not calm down until he had made a vow on his makeshift shoes to liberate mankind from similar problems.

For the next 84 days, he was little use to the bank, channelling his energies into secret nightly experiments in his home workshop. That was how long it took him to create a button surrogate that he would later attempt to launch at the Columbia World's Fair as 'the latest wonder from the world of technology'. He had succeeded in acquiring two patents: No. 504037 and No. 504038, dubbed the 'clasp locker and unlocker for shoes'.

At the Fair, a young lawyer named Lewis Walker stumbled across Judson's exhibit. A gadget that replaced buttons and clasps – brilliant! Walker slammed down 500 dollars to buy Judson's invention and founded the Universal Fastener Company. His bank was initially reluctant but good friends supplied Walker with working capital.

Only to discover that Judson's invention was practically worthless.

Ingenious, to be sure. But clumsy, unreliable and expensive to produce. Within a short time, Judson received a desperate letter from Walker, offering immediate employment. Overjoyed, Judson began work in his new workshop, pay-check courtesy of Walker, only to recognise, after months of hammering, sawing, filing and puzzling, that he must be incompetent. The clasp could not be fixed. With a heavy heart he gave up, declared his invention worthless, and returned to the bank.

'Mankind is stuck with its awkward chunks of bone and button,' he seemed to reason. 'If God had wanted us to have zippers, He would have installed them right from the beginning.'

Right across Whitcomb L. Judson's big mouth, for starters.

But Lewis Walker was anything but a quitter; by now he had adopted the title of Colonel and had acquired a taste for commanding troops. And he was not about to give up his presumptive commercial empire. He was still convinced that the zipper was a great idea. On

Peter A. Aronsson and his daughter Elvira, circa 1905. Aronsson himself did development work on the zip fastener, but his main contribution was in headhunting the gifted Gideon Sundbäck. In 1909 he also became Sundbäck's father-in-law when Elvira married the up and coming young engineer from Småland.

Whitcomb L. Judson's 1896 prototype – created in frustration on a day when everything was going wrong.

1,219,881.

Patented Mar. 20, 1917.

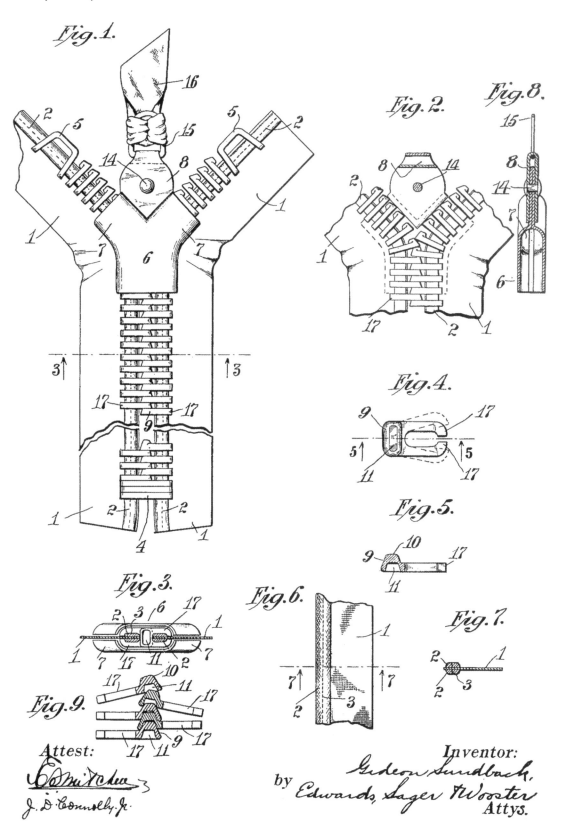

Fig. 1.

Fig. 2.

Fig. 8.

Fig. 4.

Fig. 5.

Fig. 6.

Fig. 7.

Fig. 3.

Fig. 9.

Attest:
C. C. Mitchell
J. D. Connolly, Jr.

Inventor:
Gideon Sundback,
by Edwards, Sager & Wooster
Attys.

22

the other hand, he had begun to view Judson as a charlatan. He set out to find a real inventor and enquiries shortly led him to a smart Swede called Otto Fredrik Gideon Sundbäck, employed as an engineer by Westinghouse in Chicago.

Gideon Sundbäck was a self-made man, sprung from the rocky soil of Småland. He was born in 1880 in a one-horse town that survived on its coach-making business, turning instead to furniture-making when the motor car made its entry. Gideon Sundbäck's father, Jonas, was a prosperous forestry owner, able to afford to send his son to study abroad. So Gideon studied electronic engineering in Berlin, Sachsen and Bingen in Germany, graduating in 1903. He acquired the reputation of being good at study, with a nose for business. The young man liked to dress well, perhaps even to the point of snobbishness. His well-fed face was decorated with a little, downy black moustache, a bow-tie often perched under his double chin. He was in many ways an impressive character.

Attired in a black suit, Sundbäck arrived in the United States in 1905. Not long afterwards Sundbäck ran into a countryman, Peter A. Aronsson, who had worked in a mechanical workshop at a steel mill back home. At the time, Aronsson was chief henchman for the mildly nutty but nonetheless impressive 'Colonel' Walker.

'We're working on an invention that will replace buttons,' said Aronsson.

'Good luck,' replied Sundbäck.

'What I'm saying is, the Colonel could use an intuitive, imaginative brain like yours.'

'You're right, he must be crazy!'

Sundbäck was affronted. Spend time and money on a replacement for buttons? You couldn't find a more stupid invention. Besides, his field was electrical, not mechanical, engineering. He made generators, not hooks and eyes. He could probably put together a passable lightning conductor, but to spend time on buttoning women's corsets … Luckily, he thought, he already had a job, a good one in a Chicago office. So he didn't have to work for knuckleheads and dummies.

But Aronsson kept babbling. And when he told Colonel Walker about his gifted compatriot, Walker, for some reason, jumped at the chance. Perhaps he saw something no one else did. Perhaps he was simply desperate. After three letters to Sundbäck had failed to prompt

The revolutionary 1917 patent. Gideon Sundbäck's invention was called the 'separable fastener' and differed in one important aspect from all similar, earlier models – it worked!

a reply, he travelled to Chicago and walked right into Sundbäck's office suite.

'He's gone back to Sweden,' lied the secretary.

'Then he'll catch cold on the way,' replied Lewis, happily pointing at the coat-rack with Sundbäck's winter coat dripping sleet onto the floor.

He pushed his way into the office, where the guilty Sundbäck was hunched over his desk. Within minutes, the two men had become friends for life and allies in the Great Mission to redeem mankind from its grievous daily annoyances:

- the shoelace that always breaks when you are most in a hurry
- the button flies that always pop open when you are having dinner with the boss
- the corset that always gets stuck when there is a taxi waiting

'Our latest invention is called C-CURITY,' said Walker, and Sundbäck recalled the press advertisement:

One tug and it's done!
No more open skirts!
No old-fashioned hooks-and-eyes or buckles
Your skirt is always safely and attractively closed
C-CURITY
Slit-proof
Ask the girl!

Why not ask the girl? It was the fair sex that ultimately set the stage for the zipper revolution, and it was a special girl, Aronsson's daughter Elvira, who finally got Sundbäck to settle in America. A year after quitting his job with the generator manufacturer, Sundbäck married Elvira. They set up house in Hoboken, then a dull backwater in New Jersey, though not far from New York City.

Every extra penny Walker made at the law office went to the workshop, to be swiftly swallowed by a range of experiments. It was money down a Black Hole. Debts piled up apace with the dust on the fastener prototypes crowding the shelves. There was always something wrong; the machines jammed, got stuck, loosened, rusted or fell off their attachments.

An early advertisement for the American zip manufacturer Talon, one of two offshoots from the Sundbäck empire. But the zip fastener was not an overnight success; a world war and a number of debonair soldiers were needed to alert the general public to its practical use.

On and off so easily... always trim and smooth

It's closed with a **TALON** Reg U S Pat Off *fastener*

AKG

Then, Sundbäck met his life's first tragedy: Elvira died in 1910 in childbirth. Their daughter, Ruth, survived, but was sent back to Sweden to live with Sundbäck's mother and father in Småland, where she remained until the age of 17. Sundbäck buried his sorrow in work and redoubled his experiments.

It still took three years.

But then one day in 1913, Sundbäck was to exclaim: 'Walker, we've done it!' The two men promptly marched off to a bar to celebrate, arms around each other's shoulders. By accounts, it was a long and wet night. Time and again, they toasted each other and the invention that would conquer the world. They could hardly wait until dawn – their ingenious product must quickly be put into production.

The product was inspired, no question. Sundbäck had taken Judson's idea and cross-fertilised it with a newly patented, but unmarketed, Swiss invention. Their new fastener had more and denser segments and more points of contact. The old zipper looked like a giant's dentures – now, every 'tooth' was only a fifth, or even a tenth, as big. The new zipper was far more supple and flexible. And it did not pop apart as easily.

Sundbäck had built machines to punch out teeth and clip them onto ribbons of cloth. Until now, this had been done manually.

Universal Fastener was ready to pump out the zippers and the partners, Walker & Sundbäck, waited excitedly for an invasion of customers.

But the market was quiet.

Dead quiet.

After years of sub-standard slide fasteners, customers had finally given up. Technology-crazy America had shown patience, but patience was at an end. There was no goodwill bank to back the invention. Not even for the Swede claiming to have invented the perfect fastener, singing its praises in these words:

Opening like a smile
closing like a line drawn on water

The poetry did actually attract some enquiries: a few toy manufacturers and that magician with the rabbits, who saw the zipper as an entertaining novelty.

Four more years passed. In Europe, the First World War was raging. Sundbäck and Walker started preparing for bankruptcy. One morning, when their secretary brought them the morning mail, she happened to mention that one letter appeared not to be a bill but an order!

A master tailor called M.S. Groom in Brooklyn wanted 1,500 small zippers.

'What the hell does he want to use them for?' mumbled Sundbäck.

'Let's go and find out,' replied the vigorous Walker.

To be honest, they were not especially busy. Once at the tailor's, they were told that seamen wanted the zippers.

'It's for something useless, really,' said the tailor. 'Sailors want zippers on their wallets. They think it's the latest admiralty fashion.'

Admirals? Sundbäck and Walker asked if they could wait in the shop for a while. When some sailors showed up, the inventors stepped forward.

'How would you like to be able to open and close your duffle backs with a zipper? Or your windcheaters? Wouldn't that be grand?'

When the seamen agreed, the dynamic duo dashed off to Navy HQ and snagged their first million-dollar deal. The Universal Fastener Company suddenly had the war industry as its main customer source. Zippers sewn into airmen's jackets were a huge success, keeping bodies warm in freezing cockpits.

In Europe, people stared wide-eyed at the cunning way American soldiers buttoned their clothes. When the war ended orders dropped off, but by then other customers were already lining up. One was the B.F. Goodrich Company, then principally a shoemaker, which signed a huge order for zippers for sports shoes. Other customers wanted zippers for tobacco pouches, gloves and, from 1930, men's trousers.

Even the name accelerated. A British company, Kynoch Ltd, bought the European manufacturing rights from Sundbäck and renamed the product 'lightning fastener', which quickly caught on. In 1923, another British shoemaker company dubbed its galoshes the 'Zip Boot', producing the now-venerable nickname, 'zipper'.

With Walker pulling back more and more, Gideon Sundbäck's name and the zipper's development became indivisible. He remarried, this time taking his secretary Marguerite, the daughter of a Baptist minister. Their children were Paul, Dick and Erik; the first two were later to become engineers with their father's company while Erik became a town planner in Washington. In 1925, the zipper empire divided into two halves – Lightning Fastener Co and Talon Incorporated – which dominated the world market.

Sundbäck's daughter, Ruth, returned to the United States and married a native of Göteborg, John Klingener, who was then promoted to head the Tanlon factory in Canada.

Interestingly, Ruth's grandfather, Peter Aronsson, remained on the scene. For a few intensive years he became his son-in-law's greatest business rival. In 1910, perhaps in connection with Elvira's death or perhaps to take little Ruth back to Sweden, he moved to Europe and started a zipper factory in Paris. Aronsson's zippers were the first to reach the Swedish market. The general agent was a Swede who had spent some time in Paris, Alfred Zetterberg. He called the zipper 'le Ferme-Tout Américain'. (Almost a hundred years later, Swedish still uses a corrupted version of the name, fermitet, to mean speed, although the French root means to close.)

The first Swedish zipper advertisement dates from 1912: 'Lucky husbands! The hour of liberation is at hand. A Swedish-American, A.P. Aronsson, has had the excellent notion of inventing a quick-buttoner, by the use of which ladies can dress themselves, that is, button up their backs.'

Further down, the copy noted the usefulness of the invention for the defence forces. It was suggested that the military use the zipper to 'swiftly and safely secure tent sections'.

But problems quickly arose. The instructions were long and hard to understand: 'One grasps the ring in one's right hand, while with the left holding tight the lower extremity of the apparatus, dragging it from down to up. If, in the process, the slide sticks, then neither shake nor tug but open again, slightly, dragging the while, and the apparatus should work excellently.'

One plan was to sell zippers to the Royal Dramatic Theatre, where swift changes of clothes were needed. The theatre did in fact buy a few, and one of the great actors of the Swedish stage, Anders de Wahl, was among the first guinea-pigs.

Another prospective customer was the Swedish postal service. Aronsson painted a glowing picture of zippers on mailbags streamlining the work of mail deliverers. But the Post Office turned him down; his product was too expensive and perhaps unreliable. Aronsson faded

A French zip fastener that was on sale in Stockholm's Old Town in 1912. The zip's designer was Gideon Sundbäck's father-in-law P.A. Aronsson who had started a new career in Paris after his daughter's death.

LE FERME-TOUT

AMÉRICAIN

PERFECTIONNÉ BREVETÉ S.G.D.G.

REMPLAÇANT
les Boutons & Agrafes
dont la pose est longue
LE FERME-TOUT
procure par sa souplesse
SÉCURITÉ & RAPIDITÉ
Toute femme élégante et
pratique l'adoptera.

Elle évitera ainsi
l'ouverture fréquente et
si disgracieuse de ses
jupes et corsages. Elle
trouvera en outre toute
commodité pour s'habiller
rapidement et sans le
concours de personne.

POUR JUPES 2 Tailles

| 26 Centimètres | PRIX: | 1f25 |
| 32 | | 1f45 |

POUR CORSAGES 4 Tailles

33 Centimètres	
36	"
38	"	PRIX 1f75
40	"

SE FAIT EN NOIR, BLANC, BLEU, BRUN ET GRIS

Reklamkort för Aronssons blixtlås. Tryckt i Paris omkr. 1911. — Tillhör Tekniska Museet.

from view, and when in 1938 Stockholm's Museum of Science and Technology made a public appeal for stories about the development of the zipper, they were rewarded with an anecdote about 'an eerie character, Aronsen of Alsace', criss-crossing Europe, knocking on doors to 'flog his gadgets'. Another version had the mysterious widget-seller as a Jew. Behind this modern version of the Wandering Jew hid Peter A. Aronsson, whom the passing years had not treated gently.

In 1919, Aronsson/Aronsen returned to the United States, but his days as a zipper king were over. He lagged far behind his son-in-law in product development. Aronsson got a job at the General Electric plant in Bridgeport, Connecticut. He died in Bridgeport in the summer of 1936.

Back in the old country, a little mill in the one-horse town of Gusum had just been given a new lease of life thanks to the zipper. Ironically, it was neither Aronsson's nor Sundbäck's but a Swiss patent. But by 1938, Sundbäck's tentacles had reached Gusum as well. Soon, seven kilometres of zipper a day were being punched in the southern Swedish spruce forests. A newspaper wrote: 'The market is now worldwide, except for Africa and India, where the natives have yet to learn the use of the zipper for their more or less exotic costumes.'

The zipper means a freer existence for the working man, wrote the Swedish trade union paper 'The Metal Worker' two years later: 'It represents Life's rebellion against mercenary society, where time, money and energy are stolen from the masses by unpractical devices in different sectors.'

The zipper became Hollywood's favourite symbol for sex and eroticism. As early as 1932, the visionary writer, Aldous Huxley, had let his genetically perfect breeding women in 'Brave New World' glide out of their uniforms with a single elegant gesture, ready for love-making. And running trains into tunnels became outmoded; instead, the love act was suggested by the stealthy fingering of a dress's zipper – everybody got the picture. In the 1930s, darkened cinemas would resonate to the sound of thousands of willing zipper teeth.

The '40s experienced a zipper revolution with everything from 'sleeping bags' for idled British aeroplanes to insulating covers for children in prams. New materials such as artificial resin and polyester

The legendary 'Aronsen of Alsace', a.k.a. P.A. Aronsson (1862–1936). By the time he returned to the United States, his son-in-law Gideon Sundbäck had established an irreversible lead in product development.

were tried out but had a tendency to melt in contact with an electric iron. Swedish women were tempted with 'colourfully painted fasteners and sweet Lilliputian fasteners – so pliant and easy-to-use with all the sophisticated pocket-cuts now adorning dresses', as a wartime ad from the Gusum factory put it. But Real Men were hard to win over. Why take a chance? Why risk getting your tie stuck in your flies? It was not until the '50s that zippers were in every man's trousers.

When Gideon Sundbäck passed away at his Meadville home on 21 June 1954, he left 89 patents and 13 million dollars – an almost incredible fortune for the times. His nephew Nils Otto Sundbäck, a Stockholm school principal, gave his uncle top marks as a businessman, with a sharp intellect and a biting wit. 'The only rest my uncle got was on transatlantic trips. He always went by boat. He didn't like flying, which resulted from a flight he once took with the Wright brothers, which crashed.'

An anecdote told in passing, but a wonderful, forgotten story.

His daughter, Ruth, also testified to her father's lifelong drive to invent. She remembered a pipe used to slide firewood down to the basement, a refrigerated room for food and a new kind of paper-clip. He even created a crafty mechanism that turned cottage beds into couches for daytime use. And for the dinner table, a motorised serving trolley would buzz around, serving the guests – like something out of an old Mickey Mouse film.

When the dinner guests finally drifted off home in the late evening, a sleepy Sundbäck would be able to simply stretch out a finger and with a touch on a button, make both trolley and couches disappear.

Like a line drawn on water.

STUNTED POWER

Jonas Wenström 1855–1893

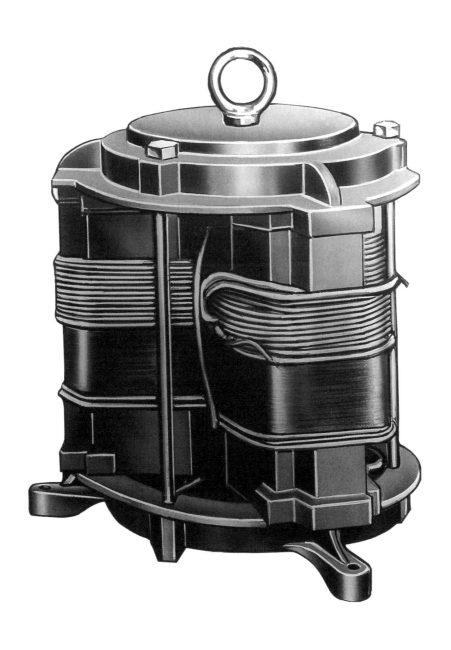

Thomas Alva Edison was taking a nap. The little cripple from Sweden waited, in vain, in Edison's laboratory.

A letter home did not divulge any frustration. For posterity remained only a laconic note that: 'My visit was nonetheless interesting, even though Edison himself was not present, since, exhausted from extensive work, he had retired to rest in his palatial villa, some distance from the laboratory.'

Their roles might well have been reversed.

In 1878, ten years earlier, Edison had become world famous for his electric light bulb, but the truth is that the patent might well have been awarded to a handicapped 23-year-old Swede.

Letter to father from the University of Kristiania (now Oslo), 25 October 1878: 'Finely distributed carbon particles that bind an electrical current (as in arc light cables) produce the most brilliant light phenomenon. Or: take a flame from a candle, a lamp, a gaslight or anything that contains glowing carbon particles. Introduce the flame between the terminals so that the current flows through the flame. Thus can the sootiest oil lamp become a clear, shining star.'

And a year later: 'Edison's new invention for electrical light, namely a glowing carbon strip, is the same as I discovered a year ago … had I then his laboratory and resources, I would have accomplished the same and better … a graphite strip between two mica plates produces a more effective light than Edison's thin, unsupported carbon wick in the airless glass bulbs.'

Jonas Wenström was to devote his entire short life to the mysteries of electricity, although his own flame was flickering.

A great darkness could be glimpsed within the man who gave Sweden light.

Always slightly too late. Never truly recognised. Jonas Wenström numbers among Sweden's least known geniuses – a sharp mind in an incomplete body. There was something truncated, something deeply tragic about the slender figure with its thin legs and stooped back.

There is a picture that reveals more than most. Six men are posing for the photographer on a forest slope. Five of them have moustaches, and all have elegant hats. They are of average height, all except the person second from the right. He resembles a child at a masquerade, a boy dressed up as an adult. The face resembles a young Nietzsche, but the body is a heron's, with abnormally thin legs and a throat that

Jonas Wenström (1855–1893) was anything but an imposing figure, but with a little more luck and cheek, could have been world famous for his work in telephony, agricultural machinery and electronics. His handicap stopped many from taking him seriously. Today, he is among Sweden's forgotten geniuses, even though his patents founded the power technology giant, ASEA.

Previous page: Wenström's first three-phase generator, called the triple generator, from the late 1880s.

seems to extend straight from the torso. The photograph was taken during Jonas Wenström's American visit in mid-1888. He travelled across on the steamship Arizona, visiting among others his long-time correspondent Thomas Edison, in Orange, New Jersey. The two men had written to each other for ten years. So it was something of a shock that Edison could not even forego his early afternoon nap to welcome his friend.

Maybe it wasn't a shock. Jonas Wenström was used to disappointment. His 33 years on earth had thus far been a struggle for recognition, perhaps even love. He had never even had a girlfriend, not to mention children. Loneliness was a yoke on his fragile shoulders. His mouth was drawn. His eyes myopically sad behind thick lenses.

There he was on American soil for the first time, perhaps thinking that he ought to be impressed by the magnificence he saw. But no. 'Besides, I observed that the electrical illumination by light bulbs, seen in comparatively very few places, was inferior in brilliance to both the equally rare gas lighting here and the light bulb illumination we are familiar with in Sweden.'

The trip was financed by a grant and the report shows that its beneficiary was appropriately observant. But there was poignancy in his frequent failure to meet those he wanted to. In New York, he sought out another inventor, Edward Weston, but: ' … unfortunately, I was unable to meet him in person, although his colleagues showed me through his exceptionally well-appointed and equipped laboratory chambers.'

' … On the 20th, I presented myself at the office of Mr Beggs, the manager of Edison's illumination stations in New York, and was given his permission to visit the stations, of which solely the old one was in operation, as the two newer stations were as yet unfinished. Mr Beggs promised to show me one of the new ones himself, but was impeded, so I went there alone on the 21st.'

Was it his handicap that allowed his hosts to treat him so casually? Jonas Wenström was no imposing figure; quite the contrary. His condition was never diagnosed but probably resulted from rickets. The growth of his entire upper body seemed to have been arrested. Jonas Wenström's father, Wilhelm, and his younger brother, Göran, were both lofty men.

It may even have been the disability that caused Jonas to become an inventor. Very early in life, he immersed himself in the world of books. Maria, his mother, would find him bent over thick tomes and his father noticed with satisfaction that the boy had inherited an interest in scientific puzzles.

With one difference.

The boy found them even easier to understand.

This became apparent when Jonas started grammar school in the city of Örebro, where Wilhelm Wenström had moved to set up a business in engineering design. Jonas's father was a master smith and a mill builder, a trade that guaranteed both rank and income in a region bubbling with activity around 1870. As well, the Wenström family knew John Ericsson, the man who had developed the screw propeller and the first armoured turret warship, the 'Monitor'. Ericsson had been an American citizen since 1844, but often wrote letters full of complex technical descriptions.

It was an inspiring friendship. Later in his own life, Jonas Wenström would initiate a private correspondence with the famous émigré. On 17 September 1877, for example, Wenström jotted down a memo on how radiation impacts and heats a surface, and sent it to Ericsson in New York.

Wilhelm Wenström, meanwhile, was building blast furnaces, water turbines and rolling mills with his eldest son, Jonas, following father's activities with great interest.

For all his life, the relationship with his father would be Jonas Wenström's most important social lifeline. 'How enjoyable it would be if Father and I had a little inventors' workshop with a laboratory, etc.,' he wrote, in February 1880. He was 27 at the time and had already invented the electric light, the threshing-mill, the cream skimmer, the telephone and the electronic ore sorter.

At least on paper.

In 1876, he commenced studies at Uppsala University, and with neither money nor laboratory, began to experiment with a dynamo, or more exactly a self-exciting direct current generator. At the time, Swedes read by kerosene light. Nowhere was the horizon broken by electricity lines.

Not that ordinary Swedes were ignorant of electricity. Everyone who had stroked a cat knew how sparks arose, how lightning worked,

The Wenström brothers, Jonas (left) and Göran, pose for the photographer in their velvet suits. Jonas's illness has yet to appear. He is a precocious child, astounding people with his astute brain and analytical capability.

Jonas's father, Wilhelm, was a constant correspondent, source of inspiration and sounding-board. Wilhelm Wenström's field was wrought iron and the construction of forging furnaces and water turbines for the expanding regional industries in Bergslagen, south-central Sweden.

how weak signals could convey messages via telegraph. At the Korsnäs-Marma sawmill, electric arc lights – the bulb's ancestry – had recently been installed, and in only two years, Blanch's Café in Stockholm would become the country's first licensed premises with electrified lighting.

The problem was how to transport large volumes of strong current over distances. Mines, forest mills, factories: everywhere there was a need for energy in bulk. Whoever could solve the problem stood to gain fame and great fortune.

In a letter from university in Kristiania, to which he had transferred, Jonas Wenström wrote of experiments with a spinning-wheel. Even at this stage, his dream of being a full-time inventor was taking shape: 'It would be exceedingly enjoyable if, at some juncture, I could earn enough to achieve complete independence like Edison, devote myself entirely to Science and set up a laboratory.'

Edison was his idol. Taking courage, he finally sent off a letter to America. It has not been preserved, although the reply has, and in it, the magician of Menlo Park, in his slangy, indirect style, expresses thanks for the brochures he has received and wonders if Jonas Wenström can do him a favour: 'May I enquire if thorium is available in any quantity in Norway – and from whom and at what price? Very truly, T.A. Edison.'

Revisionists claim that Edison got his idea for the light bulb from Wenström's letters. The American was eight years older, and an artful person. One cannot help wondering what would have happened had Jonas Wenström applied for a patent for his lamp using 'a graphite strip between two mica plates'.

Instead, he continued his natural science studies as an anonymous student, attending the opera in Kristiania in his free time. Music was his only pleasure, apart from his studies. His letters home were full of learned comments on various singers. On 4 November 1877, he noted with some amusement that 'the singers were slightly long in the tooth, in particular the male lead, who was somewhat hoarse' and that the female lead was so poor that 'I could not stifle my laughter at her bass trills'.

But Jonas was also a dutiful son who reported faithfully on his progress and worried about the family's welfare: October 9, 1877: 'I equally hope that no one at home is ill, for I would surely have

The famous Edison letter, dated 18 November 1879. 'The magician of Menlo Park' asks his 24-year-old admirer in Kristiania (now Oslo) for help in assessing the availability of the mineral, thorium. Not a word about the invention of the light bulb, whose principle Wenström claimed to have solved a year before Edison.

The dynamo affectionately known as the Corset that became one of the young ASEA company's best sellers.

Swedish inventor John Ericsson (1803–89) emigrated to America and helped the Northern states win the Civil War through his propellor-driven armoured ship, the Monitor. Ericsson's influence was great among many young Swedish inventors, not least Jonas Wenström, whose father corresponded for years with the famous Swedish-American.

Menlo Park, N. J., *Nov 18* 18/9

Jonas Wenström Esq
        Kristiana Norway
Dear Sir,
                Your favor of
the 17th ulx was duly
recd also the pamphlet
for which please accept
thanks — May I enquire if the
Mineral Thorite can be obtained
in any considerable quantity
in Norway — of whom and
at what price ?
                Very truly
                        T. A. Edison

been advised … J. Ericsson's books occupy pride of place among the others through their size and brilliance. They are so well printed and bound as to be masterpieces through that alone. For example, one can view one's reflection in the gilt edging … When Mother is to travel here, may I beg her to bring my slippers and my (repaired) winter cap?'

'Inventing is a diversion from studying,' he wrote, but was unable to hide his chagrin when, in a letter dated 1 April, he noted that a new method of telegraphy that he had refined 'years ago' had just been discovered by 'an Englishman, who has executed the idea in a far more complicated way'.

Or, on 12 May: 'Edison has invented a telephone heard over great distances through use of mechanical energy using materials, by fission, to increase the sound volume. I have therefore constructed a magnetic telephone of similar strength with no need for moistening or suchlike.'

With extremely good grades in philosophy, mathematics, English, astronomy, physics and chemistry, Jonas returned home to Örebro in the summer of 1879.

He began work as a technical consultant on his father's assignments, continuing all the while to ponder over new inventions. He was putting the finishing touches on a new navigational instrument that, using neither magnet nor sextant, would be able to give exact latitude and longitude 'from any spot on Earth'. He also looked up a family friend, mill owner G.A. Engelbrektsson, offering to build him a direct-current motor to light the mill.

But the mill owner refused.

'It's basic mechanics, Jonas. If you can think up a rotary machine with a horizontal axle driven by a belt, something like the Grammes machine we had here last winter, then I'd be happy to help you experiment with it in the mill workshop.'

The words were lodged in his brain as he journeyed to the Paris World Exhibition of 1881. All around him were inventions he now realised would never survive in use. They were ingenious but fragile. He was especially attentive to dynamos, judging that none would survive the stress and strain of factory work. Electricity had a future, he realised, but the business was riddled with crackpots.

Wenström spent three months as a trainee at a mechanical firm in Frankfurt, and when he returned to Örebro, he was armed with

Jonas Wenström's ingenious generators were one of the keystones for Sweden's expanding industrial economy and, not least, for the nascent multinational, ASEA, now ABB. In his short life, Wenström built numerous models of different size and strength.

The Arboga factory's 'lightning bugs'. To the left of the direct-current motor is G.A. Rehlin, the man who saved Jonas Wenström's first significant electrical invention, the Tortoise, by snipping off the grounding wire. The tall, bearded man to the left of centre is 'Big Lars', a man of legendary strength.

The first Swedish dynamo, the Tortoise, the work of Jonas Wenström. It is not hard to guess where it got its nickname.

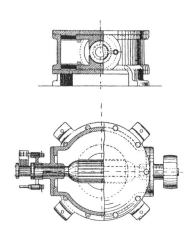

enough expertise to meet the reluctant mill owner's demands.

The new generator was dubbed the Tortoise. Throughout the spring and summer of 1882, Wenström worked on his rare reptile in the mill workshop and by August, he was ready to demonstrate.

It would not even turn over.

Carl Engelbrektson, the mill owner's son, would later describe how his father's patience shortened as the weeks went by: 'Finally, he gave Jonas an ultimatum: "If the lights aren't on by Monday at noon, you'll have to dismantle your motor and continue work somewhere else!" Monday came, and still no current. At noon, my father marched off home, bristling with anger, and I heard a rumour that when Jonas left, he was crying. Ten minutes later, the mill was lit up by the most magnificent illumination anyone had ever seen. What had happened? Well, when Rehlin was left there alone, he started thinking about the connections. In particular, there was a grounding wire he thought unnecessary, since the electricity, according to Wenström, went from the motor through one of the copper brushes – through the lamps – and back to the other copper brush. What was the earth wire good for? He promptly snipped the wire with his pliers, and it happened.'

The redeeming angel, mechanic G.A. Rehlin, was Wenström's assistant at the mill. Thanks to Rehlin's inspired move, Wenström was able to negotiate a contract with the major electricity player of the time, Ludvig Fredholm of Stockholm.

Fredholm was a banker turned wholesaler. While travelling in England in 1880, he was struck by the splendid qualities of electric lighting. His assistant was a certain Göran Wenström, an engineer from Örebro. 'You ought to meet my elder brother,' Göran used to entreat his chief. 'His name is Jonas and he is a genius.'

(As an aside: this was only one example of how Fredholm influenced Swedish history, almost involuntarily. The other was when Fredholm's precarious business dealings happened to bankrupt a young Stockholmer. Destitute, the young man threw himself into the writing of a novel, which was published in 1879 as 'The Red Room'. The young man's name was August Strindberg.)

Ludvig Fredholm and Göran Wenström journeyed to Örebro to demonstrate light bulbs. It was the beginning of an intensive tug-o'-war between gas and electricity. Every town in the country had to

Ludvig Fredholm, wholesale trader with an interest in technology. He jump-started Jonas Wenström's career in electricity, but would later block many of Wenström's other inventions.

Jonas Wenström's younger brother Göran who became factory manager at Arboga and Ludvig Fredholm's partner.

In a vacant loft in the town of Arboga, five men were set to work making electrical apparatuses under brother Göran Wenström's supervision. The town held its breath, waiting for the promised wonder of electric light.

make a choice. Fredholm charmed Örebro by rigging light bulbs on the city's main bridge and in the theatre's huge chandelier during the festive January Market.

'The light, enclosed in an opalescent bulb,' wrote the local newspaper, 'is clear and beautiful, tending towards mauve and flickering only slightly. The gas flames alongside appear, in comparison, extremely humble.'

It was here that Fredholm met the elder Wenström brother.

The result of their meeting was that Fredholm bought Jonas Wenström's patent and founded the Electrical Company (Elektriska Aktiebolaget) in Stockholm on 17 January 1883. The company's office was in Fredholm's Stockholm home and manufacturing took place in 44 square metres of free floor space above a workshop in Arboga, central Sweden. Five men under Göran Wenström built the generators. Among them was 'Big Lars' Larsson, a bearded giant of a man with enormous strength who quickly became known as 'the light factory's heavy crane'.

The factory's workers were known as 'lightning bugs' and were regarded with awe and some fear by the townspeople. When the town installed electric lighting in August 1889, the local newspaper wrote: 'Everything shipshape! Full speed ahead! And a flood of light descended on our little community, both indoors and outdoors. The old street lamps were irrevocably doomed to lesser status; some electricity subscribers were forced from their homes, having furnished themselves with lamps that were too large. The entire town stumbled around, smitten with the electric fever.'

Jonas Wenström became Technical Adviser, and his assignment was to stay put in his father's office in Örebro and think.

It is something he did very well. The Tortoise was followed by several new direct-current motors, all with quaint names: the Pot, the Beehive and the Corset. In 1887, the generator that was to become known as the 'Wenström Well Renowned' appeared. Three hundred and twelve were built over the next 15 years.

Meanwhile, he was fine-tuning other inventions. For example, an electromagnetic ore grader was sold to the Kantorp mine company and would spread across the United States. In the same year, Wenström took out a patent on an electric oven, also used in the processing of ore into iron.

A whirring monster and a keystone support for Sweden's industrial expansion. Jonas Wenström's pioneering three-phase generator was shown at the Paris Exhibition of 1900 where it aroused attention. It was model number 6 and it packed 300 horsepower.

ASEA, born as the Elektriska Aktiebolaget in Stockholm, contributed greatly to the illumination of Swedish homes as prosperity spread. Note the ancient Aryan sun symbol, later removed from the company's advertisements when the Nazis grew to strength in Germany.

And yet, something was holding him back.

Wenström could have been another in the line of famous Swedish inventors such as Dalén or de Laval, but his inventions tended to blink and then expire like broken light bulbs. The problem was Ludvig Fredholm. He retained priority for all the company's patents but filed them away, unused. Fredholm was certainly a pioneer but his single goal was to bring light to a darkened land. Being entrusted with the illuminations for the visit of the Portuguese monarch in 1886 was a task he took to heart. Other inventions were of peripheral interest. For example, when Göran Wenström, fresh from a research tour on the Continent, suggested that the company develop power transmission, Fredholm rejected the notion. If the brothers cared to waste their time on hauling electricity to mines, railways, cableways and machinery, they would be advised to set up their own company.

They promptly did in 1889, quickly snaring a large order for an electrical railway for the Boxholm Timber Company and another for passenger traffic between Stockholm and its genteel northern suburb of Djursholm. This brought Fredholm back to his senses and in 1890, the two companies merged. A prominent businessman in the south-central city of Västerås, Oscar Fredrik Wijkman, known as 'the Godfather', offered them a suitable plot and cheap hydropower. A planned joinery factory had failed and the earmarked capital was burning a hole in the pockets of the good burghers. The move was quickly effected and at an extraordinary general meeting on 14 December 1890, the company was about to be renamed Svenska Elektriska Aktiebolaget, SEA, the Swedish Electrical Company.

Jonas Wenström, who had brought his father and sister with him in the move to Västerås, raised a hand to suggest a prefix: Allmänna. General.

ASEA was born and rapidly achieved international recognition.

But the new company was not to have an easy start. One after another, machines broke down. An employee claimed that his clothes were set on fire, even though the machines and raw materials were identical to those used in Arboga.

Jonas Wenström was called in. Squinting through his spectacles, he immediately proposed better insulation. The humidity in the new factory building was far too high. Delicate machines need dry air.

He retired hastily to his desk, the better to retain concentration

Even Sweden's Central Bank made use of Jonas Wenström's ingenuity. This is the so-called 'duckboard-motor' that serviced the bank's offices with electricity.

In 1890, 35-year-old Jonas Wenström faced his greatest challenge: transporting high-tension electricity over large distances. Three years later, he had succeeded.

Jonas Wenström
1890

2

Brains did not gather rust in the Wenström family home. Gathered around the dining-room table are Jonas's father Wilhelm, sister Kerstin and Jonas himself. New ideas for the factory were discussed, abandoned or embellished.

as he grappled with a familiar problem: how can electricity be transported over distance?

Every contemporary physicist was aware that to reduce energy loss you needed high tension. In 1882, Marcel Deprez had moved electrical current via a high-tension cable between Miesbach and Munich, but the result was disheartening. The cable was carrying 1,600 volts, but the received energy was equivalent to half of one horsepower.

The crux was direct current itself. DC cannot be transformed upward. Alternating current, on the other hand, can be changed into high voltage, transported, and then stepped down to lower voltages to suit machinery, for example.

Jonas Wenström was in the throes of inventing three-phase power. Ingeniously, he could not transmit three times the effect by simply adding another cable. With direct current, four extra lines would be needed

Jonas Wenström's patent was registered and approved in July 1891. It had only one failing.

It didn't work.

ASEA picked up the patent, but with misgivings. The company had become accustomed to Jonas Wenström supplying smart ideas, but the three-phase system seemed to be as obstinate as the first Tortoise. Management suffered an attack of nerves. In 1891, a contract had been signed for delivery of Sweden's first long-range power transfer. The distance was 13 kilometres, between Hellsjön Lake and the mines at Grängesberg. Water turbines at the lake would power six generators.

Everything hung on Jonas Wenström's invention.

Just as with the generator in the mill, the inventor's luck was out. He had done research and development calmly and methodically. Now, he seemed to suffer a strange kind of performance anxiety. He could no longer recognise what should be obvious.

Finally, a young chief designer, Ernst Danielsson, a recent recruit, stepped forward with a solution. Wenström's motor had an easily rectified fault; a tiny adjustment and suddenly it worked like a clock. The linchpin for ASEA's expansion was in place. On Monday, 18 December 1893, three-phase power was transported along the line to Grängesberg, and people gathered to welcome the great little inventor, on his way by train.

But he was never to arrive.

Construction of a power station at Hellsjön in the spring of 1893. Thirteen kilometres away in the forest, the Grängesberg mine was impatiently waiting for Jonas Wenström's invention to supply electricity.

Sweden's first electric locomotive was built in 1891 and would serve for many years at the Wermbol Pulp Factory.

Next page: 'inside' the Hellsjön power station. Six water-driven turbines delivered electricity to the mine without power loss, using Wenström's three-phase system.

Jonas Wenström had a cold when he boarded the train for Grängesberg. It seemed inconsequential at first but his fragile body reacted violently. Struck with a high fever, he stayed on the train and continued to Västerås and home, where he was put to bed and quickly lost consciousness.

Three days after laying one of the most important foundation stones for Sweden's industrial expansion, Wenström died of inflammation of the lungs, only 38 years old.

This was Jonas Wenström's ultimate fate: to die in the final stretch. To be robbed of limelight and fame and die, coughing, in bed, while his invention was propelling the world into a new age.

In more tangible terms, the company he had helped found over a mill-wheel would later grow to a global empire with 215,000 employees in more than 30 countries.

Not even his obituary would be uncontested. For seven decades, professors were to bicker over Jonas Wenström's significance for the development of electricity. Was he really the father of the three-phase system? The Americans claimed that Nikola Tesla was first through his 1888 patent. The Germans argued for their own Michael von Dolivo-Dobrowolsky, who also took out a patent for a three-phase motor that same year.

Final judgement would not be delivered before 1959.

At that time, the German electrical engineering association, VDE, announced that after lengthy discussions, their own committee had decided on a winner: Michael von Dolivo-Dobrowolsky. There was a whiff of petty nationalism about the decision. Jonas Wenström would have to make do with something akin to an honorary mention. He was, when all is said and done, alone in creating a complete system for alternating current. It was a stroke of genius, but approximately as glamorous as being the first sprinter under 10 seconds for the hundred metres when it is revealed that somebody else had run even faster in another race two hours previously.

If Jonas Wenström had been alive, he would presumably have scratched his moustache thoughtfully and noted in his next letter to his father that, 'The committee's decision was, all in all, an interesting one.'

He was used to that.

Jonas Wenström would not live to experience his own fame. He died of lung inflammation at the age of 38 – only three days after his triumph with three-phase electricity transference at the Hellsjön power station. Wenström's inventive patents were the intellectual capital that launched a multinational company that today employs more than 130,000.

PRINCE OF THE BALL

Sven Wingquist 1876–1953

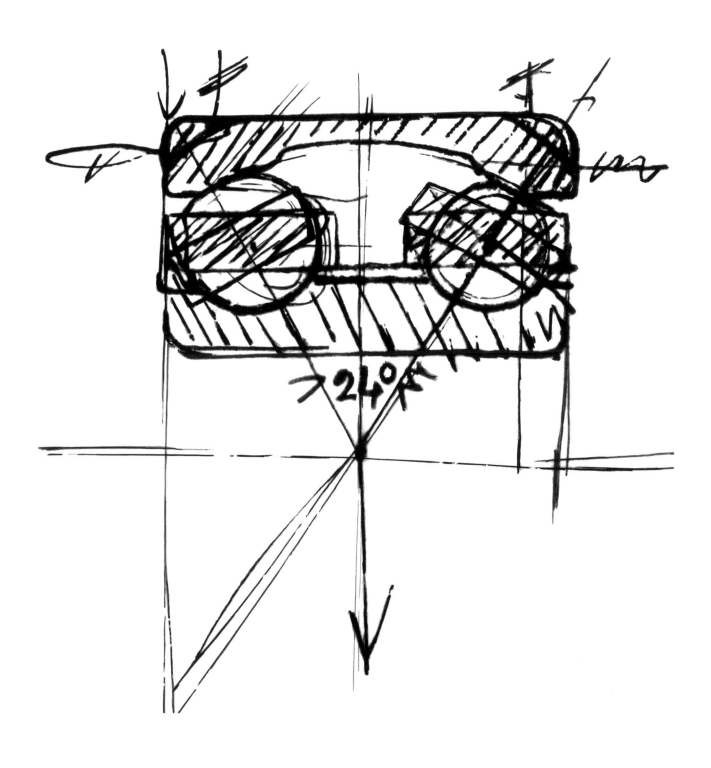

The man was meant to be a genius inventor, but looked more like a beached fisherman with his knitted sweater, sou'wester with upturned brim and spiky moustache.

The vehicle was meant to be a truck, but trundling through the forest, it seemed more like a junkyard rattletrap, a clanking jalopy with disproportionately large headlights and a dinky little rubber horn resting on the driver's lap.

The cargo consisted of woven baskets filled with sandwiches, cold cuts and ale. Along the ditches by the road, wide-eyed farmers and their cattle stared at the expedition; straight stretches of road allowed the vehicle to reach speeds of up to 35 kilometres an hour – a true wonder for the country gentry!

The real miracle was that this mobile hulk held together at all.

It really shouldn't have. Trucks of 1909 vintage had a vague, almost malevolent character. You could get them to start sweetly and chug away with important deliveries, but they often tended to stutter to a stop at the first bend.

The bearings were prone to seize up.

To be sure, ball-bearings were used as early as in the days of Caligula, as a primitive tool to get a jointed axle to turn. But little had happened in almost two millennia. Ball-bearings appeared, were put to use, then disappeared again. There was little development; it was enough that they could temporarily reduce friction. Then, under pressure, they would disintegrate. They could be handy for a bicycle, but hardly in a truck.

Take an ordinary factory at the end of the 19th century: power often came from blade wheels, belts and crankshafts. If the crankshafts were not perfectly straight, all the lubrication in the world would not help. Friction took over; the bearings overheated and the machine would have to be stopped before flames arose.

Sven Wingquist, the stationmaster's son, was well aware of all this.

Countless times he had seen his bosses curse obstinate machinery in the textile factory in Gamlestaden district in Göteborg where he worked as an engineer. Ground subsidence was another severe annoyance. And every shutdown was expensive. Ball-bearings were in short supply, and they were not made in Sweden. The best came from Germany, but delivery could take months.

And often, as soon as they were installed they would start smoking.

Sven Wingquist (1876–1953) was a stationmaster's son. Modest to a fault, he preferred to let his inventions do the talking. When manager of SKF, the Swedish Ball-bearing Company, he was a kind of ball-bearing himself, around which everything spun. He was foreman, idea-generator, travelling salesman and curator in one imposing personality.

Previous page: Sven Wingquist's own sketch of the double-tracked ball-bearing that came into being over Easter in 1906 and that founded a global industry.

Some inventions are born from vision, from the ancient dream of flying, moving, journeying, changing. But mostly, they derive from a necessity. They're practical, produced almost on the hop and providing immediate benefit to a lot of people. Not seldom, the spur is impatience and irritation.

The ball-bearing was such an invention.

Not that Sven Wingquist was an impatient man. On the contrary, he was an uncommonly quiet and sensible boy from the moment he was born on 10 December 1876 to the railway inspector in Hallsberg and his wife. Sven was the perfect son, a polite, well-mannered, industrious young man and a joy to his parents, a boon companion for his brothers and sisters and scant trouble for his teachers.

Posterity knows little of Sven Wingquist's early years. We do know he sought work in the textile industry, then in rapid expansion in rural Västgötaland province, close to Wingquist's birthplace. He graduated at the age of 18 from a technical college in Örebro and enrolled that same autumn, 1894, in the John Lenning Weaving College in the city of Norrköping.

It may sound like a hothouse for seamstresses but John Lenning College dispensed a thorough technical education, tailor-made to fit the textile industry's needs. Engineers were needed to build and develop new machines. Sven Wingquist was quick to learn and a remarkably pleasant young man. That was certainly the opinion of a relative, L.J. Wingquist, a textile manufacturer of importance in the region. No sooner had the young man left school than he was whisked away to one of the elder Wingquist's factories, then undergoing considerable expansion.

In the 17th and 18th centuries, it was part of every Swedish noble's education to spend a year travelling on the Continent, observing and learning. By the late 19th century, there was a new species of aristocrat: the young engineer sent off to learn his trade and languages and absorb the new trends, of which only rumours had reached the far North.

It was in fact a kind of petty industrial espionage. Factory doors were still wide open for visitors. People were open and expansive, caught up in the spirit of an age when all progress, however arrived at, was beneficial.

In 1896, the United States was still the place to go for new

Ball bearings were already in use in the age of the mad Roman emperor Caligula, but apparently worked unreliably. The thoughtful Sven Wingquist pondered a little deeper than most; his spherical, double ball-bearings were a godsend for factory owners fighting a losing battle against ground subsidence and uneven crankshafts. An end, finally, to inventory collapsing in smoke.

expertise. This applied in Sven Wingquist's case as well, and the 19-year-old drew up a route and a schedule for visits to textile factories. He was a dashing, broad-shouldered young man, well tailored – in his business, you had to be – but happy to venture into each factory's innards, knee-deep in oilcans and rags. He was vastly curious: How does all this work? How do you build a conveyor belt? How do you avoid costly down time?

Cheerful Americans gave him the answers. Efficiency was one of their mottoes: it cost money to have broken machinery standing idle and money was a very central concept.

Three years later, Sven Wingquist was a line engineer at the Gamlestaden textile factory on the banks of the Säve River, near Göteborg. Production management quickly realised they had a bright one on their hands. He was immediately awash in spindles, warping machines, crankshafts and turbines, charged with making it all work as smooth as silk.

Something else was flowing smoothly: alongside the factory, the river was chewing away at the clay banks and causing the building to shift a millimetre or so every now and then.

Machines would suddenly overheat without apparent reason and it almost always turned out to be because an axle had become slightly bent due to foundation shift.

Easter of 1906 presumably involved the usual Easter eggs, but Sven Wingquist, now 29, would remember it for an entirely different reason.

His draft sketches were as neat as everything else about the man, and they indicated that he must have been fine-tuning his invention for some time. His pen had evidently scuttled across the papers, paused at a problem, solved it, and danced on. The books he had devoured on the subject revealed that ball-bearings were older than he thought; that their origin was in Roman times, but that they never enjoyed wide success until 1869, when the ball-bearing became the nub of a new invention: the velocipede. The brains behind the invention was the German, Ernst Sachs. A giant factory in Schweinfurt was already hard at work feeding demand in the burgeoning industry.

Sven Wingquist's brainstorming culminated on that Easter Sunday, and when evening came, he was still at his drawing board.

The first SKF factory in Göteborg, 1907. The closest neighbour was an old artillery captain who finally moved out, incensed by the noise. This suited Sven Wingquist, happy to move in and be close to his beloved, boisterous machines.

King Gustaf V paid a visit to SKF and Sven Wingquist on 5 September 1917. The King was said to appreciate the inventor's mild, purposeful manner.

Next page: It may look like an Orwellian nightmare but in 1946, SKF was a modern factory that took good care of its employees. Sven Wingquist irritated fellow industrialists by instituting the four-week annual holiday as early as 1913. His workers also had a shorter working week and even exclusive use of a holiday island.

'Double the number of balls – that's the solution!' he triumphantly informed his boss when the factory was back at work.

'Wingquist, what are you on about?'

'The problem is that the machines are always overheating. But I've got the answer. You just need double rows of ball-bearings, an inner one and an outer. Isn't it simple?'

All the critics were merciless. Double rows of bearings! What good was that? Leading technical journals ridiculed the idea; seldom had an invention met with such solid, open scorn.

Sven Wingquist would later say that this was the best thing that could have happened.

'My competitors talked incessantly about how worthless my ball-bearings were. It made people wonder whether they might be wrong. All that extra advertising gave business a boost.'

Wingquist did not have the money to set up production. But there were several prospective investors. Two pairs of brothers – Knut and Johannes Mark, and Christopher and Axel Carlander – heard a talk by the inventor at the Technical Association and allowed themselves to be seduced by the shining steel balls, produced by the turner Oskar Olsson under Wingquist's supervision.

The new investors were brave to the point of light-headedness. No one yet knew whether there were any customers for these doubled, spherical ball-bearings. Nonetheless, Wingquist's investors plunked down a huge sum and even found an old smithy and gave the young engineer a free hand to do whatever he wanted.

On 16 February 1907, the five men met at the Gamlestaden office.

Just two days later, they formed Svenska Kullagerfabriken (the Swedish Ball-bearing Factory), SKF.

And as soon as the first ball-bearings had cooled, Wingquist packed them in a bag and set off on a demonstration tour. He was gone all of ten days, returning with a broad smile and a full order book. Often, only a brief demonstration was needed to convince factory owners.

After ten more days in the smithy, Wingquist set off on a new journey. In the first few months of SKF's existence, he visited more than 100 companies, and at most of them he met with interested people, easily convinced.

These successful tours encouraged the brothers to build a two-storey factory in Gamlestaden that summer. By October, SKF was up

Bearing up well. A finely calibrated measuring instrument checks that the ball-bearing track is accurate to within a thousandth of a millimetre. The woman was working at the Göteborg factory in 1947.

and running with twelve labourers and three administrative staff. Between 125 and 150 ball-bearings were produced a day. Outside the factory, the cantankerous old river rumbled on, only now it was aware it had met its match.

Their patent met with swift approval. It was submitted on 21 May 1907 and endorsed by 6 June. The double-rowed, spherical ball-bearing was officially an invention. For the first time, a bearing unit could automatically adjust so that 'the balls take pressure equally and so that there be no breakdown should the axle yield or be incorrectly positioned' as the patent application read.

Wingquist was welcomed everywhere he went. He said he felt the world had been waiting for his invention. His casual, friendly style also helped sell the product. He gave the impression of possessing an almost rural stubbornness, but people instinctively felt him to be honest. If his ball-bearings were of the same commendable quality, they would be worth trying.

In 1908, SKF sales were 114,000 kronor.

In 1909, 527,000.

In 1913, six million.

By 1920, 53 million.

It was a jump-start unequalled in Swedish industrial history. And Sven Wingquist was SKF's own ball-bearing: the natural centre of action. He was inventor, engineer, factory foreman and salesman in one. He travelled ceaselessly, now to the Continent, where he quickly snapped up bright young staff, and established SKF's first representation abroad in Paris, Duisburg and Helsinki. Eight years after its founding, SKF was a global empire with factories and agencies in 27 countries.

The monotonous drumming of the diesel engines and mechanical hammers had also frightened off one of the obstacles for expansion: an artillery captain who rented a nearby manor. The noise woke the captain early every morning. Desperately, he screwed his fingers into his ears, but finally was forced to capitulate and move. At which Sven Wingquist immediately took over the building, furnishing a room on the ground floor as his office and rooms above as his private apartment. The noise didn't bother him a bit – it was 'music to my ears'.

Life was just the way he wanted it. The division between work and leisure was blurred. Whenever he wanted, he could stroll over to his

A male Garbo, fled to the comfort of the forest. 'He would often walk alone, looking straight ahead,' an employee said of Wingquist. Few, if any, were close to him. In his later years, he consented to occasional interviews, but would respond almost shyly with clipped answers and truisms.

beloved factory and stroll around, pipe between his teeth, sleeves rolled up, and ready to ambush new problems.

'Problems? That's why we're here!' was a well-known Wingquist quote, and his optimism was infectious among the workers. 'The Ball' was a popular place to work. The boss was said to be a straight sort of gentleman who looked after his employees.

In 1916, on his 40th birthday, Wingquist gave his employees a present of 100,000 kronor. Ten years later, he gave them an entire little island in the Bohuslän Archipelago: beautiful Lilla Bratt Island, all 38 acres of it. And after another ten years, he donated 25,000 kronor to a fund for 'the enhancement of the summer break'. And on his 70th birthday came 2.5 million kronor for faithful service bonuses.

He was a model manager of a model factory.

He appeared tireless. Discovering problems seemed to make him even more dedicated to his goals. Bulls were to be taken by their horns, swiftly and decisively. Once, a German industrialist had laughed in his face when Sven Wingquist insisted on demonstrating his ball-bearings. The demonstration produced one of Wingquist's most loyal customers; for the rest of his life, the German would go on ordering ball-bearings from 'that pleasant Herr Wingquist'.

When his wealth bought him a house in Göteborg's snazziest district, Lorensberg, he continued to speak normally. Or rather, as normally as one could, coming from the province of Närke, Sweden's infamous 'whiner belt'. He never took on airs and always took the time to stop and talk to the men on the cutting machines.

He loved to quote Thomas Edison: 'Genius is one percent inspiration and 99 percent perspiration.' Or the anecdote about one of Edison's exhausted colleagues complaining that he'd tried 500 ways to solve some problem with the light bulb and none worked, at which Edison happily remarked, 'Wonderful! Now we know 500 ways that don't work!'

A colleague once asked Wingquist what the key to success was.

'The ability to choose competent staff.'

Another asked what skills a leader should have.

'Avoid becoming indispensable. The word itself says it all – it's impossible to promote someone who's indispensable.'

As a philosopher, he was no world-beater, but there was something modern about his ideas in a society where caps were doffed as the

A cigarette girl named Hildur lit a flame within the industrialist and became his second wife. The affair caused quite a scandal but his second marriage appears to have been harmonious to the end. The couple would often retreat to their country estate near Falköping.

manager strode by. Wingquist had colleagues whose monocles would pop out in shock at his latest exploits and who labelled him a socialist.

In 1907, SKF suddenly cut the working week to 54 hours, while most other companies still worked on 60.

In 1913, there was worse news: Wingquist decreed that his employees were entitled to four days annual holiday at full pay.

Holidays?

Industrialists across the country choked on their liqueurs. Full pay for no work at all? Preposterous!

This benefit, together with pension funds and accident insurance, was naturally a consequence of SKF's prosperity. 'Good old boss' could afford to be generous. But he also seemed better than others at reading the signs: a red wind was sweeping Europe and workers were organising, so what could be wiser than to accept the situation and steer its outcome? There was still a chance to meet Marx halfway.

One tiny scandal came to light in all those long years.

Sven Wingquist abruptly left his wife, Ester, for a young cigarette girl.

Hildur Hult was definitely a sweet young thing, and Wingquist was not the only customer to stop and chat after buying cigarettes. Wingquist was a pipe smoker, but had begun to prefer Camel cigarettes. He started buying them from Hildur and shortly, the intensive glow between them was no longer from tobacco.

The couple married. The press was notably respectful of the love affair. No newspaper wanted to offend one of Sweden's most successful industrialists. Nobody was prepared to intrude. When Wingquist abruptly resigned as SKF's general manager in 1919, it was sensational news, but nobody tried to poke into the reasons. Was the board unhappy with a manager who was more inventor than administrator? Had he been too generous with the staff?

Public respect for Sven Wingquist remained staunch, especially when in 1933 he was made manager of the venerable weapons manufacturer, Bofors. Few interviews were printed, and interviewers fought to show deference.

In Nya Dagligt Allehanda for 6 December 1936: 'Please forgive the intrusion at this late hour – it is almost 11pm – but we'd be

An unusual hobby. After retiring as general manager, Sven Wingquist devoted considerable time and energy to measuring forestry area using aerial photography.

grateful for a statement on the occasion of your approaching sixtieth birthday, Dr Wingquist!'

'This is a request for an interview?'

'In a word, yes.'

'One must be polite to the press, otherwise there'll be consequences,' was the jovial answer from the still youthful and energetic Bofors manager and founder of SKF. 'But to be honest, I would rather not.'

'But surely there's something you could say about the global activities of SKF...'

'My SKF work is largely over, and anyway, whatever I may have accomplished there is up to others to appraise.'

'Whatever I may have accomplished ...'

It was typical Wingquist. He would sidestep elegantly, ducking questions and turning attention to the company and the Great Invention.

In his later years, Wingquist would occasionally allow photographers to visit his farm property, where he would show off his latest hobby: surveying forestry by aerial photography. But he always seemed to be turning his back to the press camera and crouching over his drawing table when pictures were to be taken.

It would be up to the writer to make something of the situation, describing how 'the broad-shouldered man moved swiftly over the icy slopes that led down to Falköping township. Chilly gusts flapped at his plus-fours, but even when the gusts became nasty, they could not slow his pace. There was something symbolic in this.'

Sven Wingquist patted his fox-terrier and with an elegant wave of his hand dismissed any importance he may have had as board member or chairman of the Association of Swedish Industries and such companies as Svenska Flygmotor (Swedish Aero-Engines), Saab and Bofors. He was silent when it was pointed out that his ideas had contributed directly to the expansion of the city of Göteborg. When his French Legion of Honour decoration was mentioned, he modestly sank his gaze.

In the meantime, SKF had become a transnational company. The ball-bearings were continually being redesigned and new uses for them found: trains, machinery and construction. In 1950, three years before Wingquist's death at the age of 76, SKF had 18 factories and 31,000 employees around the world.

'Doctor Wingquist, I presume?' In 1921, SKF's general manager was summoned to the United States to receive an honorary doctorate from a technical college in New Jersey – in the same town where the Swedish inventor of the zip fastener, Gideon Sundbäck once lived. Sven Wingquist had been in America when only 19, researching ideas factory by factory.

Quizzed on the main reason for SKF's achievements, Wingquist answered 'Swedish steel'. SKF's purchase in 1916 of the Hofors steel mill and its iron ore mines was of decisive importance, he said. There had been a furnace at Hofors since 1561, which was a guarantee that SKF would never want for the best raw materials and be able to live up to its world-famous motto: 'SKF – the right bearing in the right place.'

Once, he actually found something he admired about himself: 'You can't be afraid of work. Exhaustive study is better than waiting around for a brainwave. I grew up with industry, looked into problems in-depth, but mainly I have been industrious – that will produce results sooner or later.'

One of the most sensational of those results was actually little more than a by-product, a novelty item, one of Wingquist's impulses. But in time, this novelty would conquer the world.

The origin was a competition organised by Sweden's Royal Automobile Club. The year was 1909 – and this is where we again meet that odd truck and its cute rubber horn. Under the competition rules, trucks of different makes were to travel through southern Sweden for six days. It was an endurance trial. The results would obviously help customers in their choice of truck.

Scania was the only truck company operating locally that did not enter.

The Scania was also the only Swedish-made truck equipped with Sven Wingquist's ball-bearings.

The reason for not entering was that all trucks were on order; the company simply did not have one to spare. Scania countered by announcing its own test run for the autumn. A single three-tonne truck would drive non-stop, fully loaded, from Malmö in the far south up to Stockholm. It was a far tougher test than the Automobile Club's. A loaded three-tonner on poor autumn roads could be a nightmare, not least for Wingquist's renowned ball-bearings. On 2 September, the crew set off: five men bundled up in thick woollen sweaters and heavy overcoats, on their very own Swedish Rally.

The number-plate read M108, the headlights lit up a pot-holed road and at the back, bouncing along like a puppet on a string on the rock-hard suspension, sat Sven Wingquist. 'He used to plough straight ahead all on his own,' a shop steward called Bror Nilsson once

A quiet smoke at a photo session with Lennart Nilsson. Sven Wingquist often hid behind aphorisms and quotations or behind the smoke of a cigarette or pipe. He was known to have praised himself only once: 'I was never afraid of work.'

commented admiringly. But this was a winding, twisting odyssey through moose forests and sloppy mud.

The journey took 33 hours and 39 minutes. The average speed was 20.7 kilometres an hour. There were neither accidents nor incidents. One of the participants, an engineer called Svensson, later noted with pleasure that 'the speed was, considering the total weight of the vehicle, and the massive rubber tyres it was fitted with, rather impressive – up to 30 to 35 kph. It is perhaps unnecessary to point out that the ball-bearings in question, and the vehicle in general, passed the test with flying colours.'

The trial itself would not have been much more than a footnote, if the only result had been to improve Scania's reputation.

That previously mentioned 'by-product' was far more interesting. As Sven Wingquist sat there in the back seat, an overwhelming fascination for cars came over him. This was to result in the world's first automatic transmission. From the beginning, there was interest in Detroit. Wingquist was already well known in the United States, with an honorary doctorate from a technical college in Hoboken, New Jersey, in 1923. A year later, interest and recognition arrived from another source: two young SKF staffers, Assar Gabrielsson and Gustaf Larson.

Gabrielsson's father was an egg salesman and Larson was born on a farm outside Örebro and, like Wingquist, had graduated from the city's technical elementary school. According to one story, Gabrielsson and Larson had met while both were waiting for a train. The two men also shared a dream: the creation of a Swedish-made automobile, built by local workers from Swedish iron and to Swedish quality standards. A prototype design was commissioned, drafted by a portrait and landscape painter, Helmer MasOlle, at the time engaged in a major portrait of Sven Wingquist. (It may be noteworthy that both car and industrialist had clean, straight features, narrow observation openings and a polished top.)

SKF's ball-bearings were obviously a key component. Thanks to that bumpy ride in 1909, their immunity to pressure forces had been established. With the automobile project on track, Gabrielsson went calling on SKF's management to see if the company would provide investment.

SKF went along for the ride.

Some were as small as wedding rings, others big enough to drive a car through. Sven Wingquist's invention, born from the frustration of dealing with a pesky riverbed, made both cars and machines spin.

An early car rally through the virgin forest. In the back seat, to the right, perches Sven Wingquist, contented that his ball-bearings can take the punishment.

On Maundy Thursday, 14 April 1926 – Easter keeps cropping up in SKF's history – the first of ten batch-produced cars glided out of the factory into the sunshine. It was ten in the morning. The sparkling blue skies over Hisingen, near Göteborg, were reflected in the polished paintwork. The only embarrassment was that the vehicle had to reverse out into the sunlight, because the gearbox had been wrongly installed. The last parts had arrived late the previous night on the train from Stockholm, putting such stress on supervisor Johan Fingal that he mounted the box backward.

The working name for the car was 'the GL' or 'the Larson'.

It was normal at the time to name cars after their makers (Ford, Rolls-Royce, Chrysler). But Sven Wingquist had another suggestion. Ten years earlier, when planning to launch a subsidiary, he had dreamt up a clever name. The company was abandoned and the name forgotten.

'For a company making ball-bearings, it was a perfect moniker, but …'

And again the industrialist smiled under his moustache.

'… what could be more fitting than to call a car the Latin for "I roll"?'

That'd be Volvo.

'The ball prince' put the whole world in a spin. Sven Wingquist went from straight-A student to clever inventor to visionary company manager. Master photographer Lennart Nilsson was one of the last to pose the aging industrialist in front of a camera. The picture was taken shortly before Wingquist's death in 1953.

FROM SAFETY MATCH TO PERPETUAL MOTION MACHINE – A CHRONOLOGY

1855 Janne Lundström develops the safety match.

1859 Alfred Nobel begins experimenting with nitroglycerin.

1863 L.M. Ericsson makes a crude telephone from a pig bladder and some bits of metal – 13 years before Alexander Graham Bell's patent.

1864 Alfred Nobel invents the detonator that makes nitroglycerin a practical explosive.

1866 Alfred Nobel invents dynamite.

1875 Alfred Nobel invents blasting gelatin.

1877 Gustaf de Laval dreams up a hovercraft that will ultimately reach a speed of 8 knots on Lake Mälaren.

1877 Jonas Wenström conceives the lightbulb – one year before Edison takes out his patent.

1877 L.M. Ericsson begins manufacturing telephones.

1877 Gustaf de Laval invents the milk separator.

1882 Jonas Wenström takes out a patent on his 'Tortoise' generator.

1887 Alfred Nobel creates cordite, an almost smoke-free gunpowder.

1888 J.P. Johansson invents the adjustable wrech.

1888 Gustaf de Laval makes his steam turbine.

1890 J.P. Johansson makes a clover threshing machine.

1891 Alfred Nobel makes the world's first aluminium boat.

1891 Jonas Wenström patents a three-phase apparatus for the transmission of alternating current.

1892 J.P. Johansson patents his adjustable wrench.

1892 L.M. Ericsson makes the first hand-held receiver for telephone subscribers.

1894 C.E. Johansson gets the idea for his precision gauges.

1896 Gustaf de Laval invents the milking machine.

1904 C.E. Johansson gets patent approval for his combination gauge set.

1905 Gustaf Dalén invents the flashing apparatus.

1906 Sven Wingquist creates the double-tracked, spherical ball-bearing.

1906 Gustaf Dalén invents AGA Mass which absorbs acetylene gas and makes the tubes more robust.

1907 Gustaf Dalén makes a working sun valve.

1913 Gideon Sundbäck creates a zip fastener that works.

1914 Baltzar von Platen has a vision which leads to the creation of the refrigerator.

1919 J.P. Johansson invents the pivot-necked Triplex lamp and opens a factory for workplace lighting.

1922 Baltzar von Platen and Carl Munters make a refrigerator with no moving parts.

1929 Gustaf Dalén launches the AGA cooker.

1941 Baltzar von Platen creates the wood-gas car.

1953 Baltzar von Platen develops a process for making artificial diamonds, later taken over by ASEA.

1958 Baltzar von Platen creates the dripless tap.

1974 Baltzar von Platen test-drives his 'revolutionary electric car'.

1977 Baltzar von Platen is refused a patent for his perpetual motion machine.

INDEX

NUMBER IN ITALICS INDICATE PICTURES.

THE PICTURES IN THE BOOK ARE FROM THE FOLLOWING ARCHIVES AND SOURCES:

the National Museum of Science and Technology collection, Stockholm; Pressens Bild, Stockholm; Aftonbladet bild, Stockholm; the Dalén Museum, Stenstorp; the Center for Business History in Stockholm, Bromma, (drawing on the archives of Electrolux, Ericsson, AGA and Alfa Laval); the Archives of Business and Commerce in Sörmland, Eskilstuna; the J. P. Johansson Society, Enköping; Lennart Nilsson; the Nobel Foundation, Stockholm; PressText, Stockholm; SKF, Göteborg; the Stockholm City Museum, Stockholm; the Match Museum, Jönköping; Dalarna County Archives; ABB, Västerås. Cover photo: AGA Laboratory on Lidingö island.